Teaching Literature

1-20

"The Anxiety of Teaching"

Photograph by Denise Applewhite

Teaching Literature

ELAINE SHOWALTER

Blackwell
Publishing

BLACKWELL PUBLISHING
350 Main Street, Malden, MA 02148-5020, USA
9600 Garsington Road, Oxford OX4 2DQ, UK
550 Swanston Street, Carlton, Victoria 3053, Australia

First published 2003 by Blackwell Publishing Ltd

14   2013

Library of Congress Cataloging-in-Publication Data

Showalter, Elaine.
Teaching literature / Elaine Showalter.
p. cm.
Includes bibliographical references and index.
ISBN 978-0-631-22623-9 – ISBN 978-0-631-22624-6 (pbk.)
1. Literature–Study and teaching (Higher) I. Title.
PN59 .S49 2003
807.11–dc21

2002006133

A catalogue record for this title is available from the British Library.

Set in 10 on 12.5 pt Galliard
by SNP Best-set Typesetter Ltd, Hong Kong
Printed and bound in Singapore
by Ho Printing Singapore Pte Ltd

The publisher's policy is to use permanent paper from mills that operate a sustainable
forestry policy, and which has been manufactured from pulp processed using acid-free and
elementary chlorine-free practices. Furthermore, the publisher ensures that the text paper
and cover board used have met acceptable environmental accreditation standards.

For further information on
Blackwell Publishing, visit our website:
www.blackwellpublishing.com

Contents

Preface and Acknowledgments		vi
1	The Anxiety of Teaching	1
2	Theories of Teaching Literature	21
3	Methods of Teaching Literature	42
4	Teaching Poetry	62
5	Teaching Drama	79
6	Teaching Fiction	88
7	Teaching Theory	103
8	Teaching Teachers	111
9	Teaching Dangerous Subjects	125
10	Teaching Literature in Dark Times	131
Conclusion: The Joy of Teaching Literature		141
Notes		144
Index		159

Preface and Acknowledgments

The first time I ever taught literature, in 1963, the students addressed me as "Teacher Elaine." It was the custom at the Quaker Friends Select School in Philadelphia, but I certainly wasn't much of a teacher then. I was taking a year off from graduate school, and although I had been exposed to a lot of professors, lectures, and seminars, no one had ever talked about what might be involved in teaching literature and few appeared to have given it much consideration. But I enjoyed teaching literature so much, and learned so much from my dedicated English department colleagues, Teacher Margaret Sheats and Teacher Margaret Bender, that I decided it was worth the drudgery of getting a PhD in order to keep on doing it on a higher level. Over the next 40 years, as I have became "Professor Showalter," and have taught undergraduates, graduate students, faculty, and alumni in the United States, Canada, Britain, and Europe, I've continued to think about what teaching literature means, both in theory and in practice. I hope I've improved; I have had the chance to learn from the best, both teachers and students.

This book is based partly on my own experience, but mainly on the ideas on teaching I've acquired and borrowed and stolen from many colleagues and friends at Rutgers, Princeton, Roehampton, the School for Criticism and Theory, the Salzburg Seminars, and the Modern Language Association (MLA). As a Phi Beta Kappa Scholar in 1993, I traveled around the US, lecturing, meeting faculty and students, and visiting classes at campuses as diverse as Birmingham Southern in Alabama, Clemson in South Carolina, Macalester in Minnesota, and Claremont in California. Best of all, I had the good fortune to hold one of Princeton's Cotsen Faculty Teaching Fellowships for three years, during which I had time to reflect on the teaching of literature while directing pedagogy seminars for graduate students in English and Comparative Literature.

In the past 40 years, a whole new vocabulary of pedagogy has developed, with distinctions between compulsory and post-compulsory education, young and adult learners, Bloom's taxonomy of learning objectives, Kolb's cycle of learning modes, and Dale's learning cones. But while there are now many books about pedagogy, most offer broad and generic advice about lecturing, leading discussions, course design, and grading, without specific application to a field. And while there are some books that are field-specific, and that address the teaching of literature, most are about critical interpretation rather than pedagogical process, and few have any relation to the new research being done on learning.

Most practical studies of teaching English emphasize writing rather than literature. As George Levine, one of the most eloquent diagnosticians of our current malaise, notes, "insofar as there have been serious efforts to think through teaching, they have been largely about the teaching of composition . . . The question of pedagogy gets attached, in most instances, to the teaching of writing, and the institution as a whole remains doggedly loyal to the patterns of literary training."[1] There have been many debates about the literary canon, and about the teaching of literary theory, but almost none about the day-to-day life of the literature classroom. Although we talk a lot about *what* we teach, we are embarrassed or afraid to ask *why* and *how* we teach.

This book is different. It is about real teachers in real classrooms, facing the questions and problems that don't get discussed – the anxiety dreams, the students who won't talk or can't talk, the days when we can't talk ourselves. Every experienced teacher knows that the best-laid designs and pedagogical plans are changed by the unexpected accidents and events that occur in the daily life of the classroom. I have steered away from abstract and idealistic recommendations about classroom practice, and towards accounts of what English teachers actually do. My emphasis throughout is on teaching as an activity as well as a philosophy. But I have also read the extensive research coming from educational psychology, and applied it to the special situation of teaching literature at university level. A list of the most useful books on teaching is included in chapter 1, under the section on Lack of Training.

I believe that literature itself shapes our teaching practice, or could. Levine ⟩ suggests that our profession "badly needs a whole new orientation toward the question of the relation between teaching and scholarship, and a whole new genre that would make it possible to see discussions of teaching as integral to the development of knowledge."[2] This book is my effort to respond to Levine's challenge. There are many ways to be a good teacher, but I do think that active and interactive subject-centered learning makes the most sense for teaching literature, and that the genres of drama, poetry, fiction, and theory, with their emphases on performance, memory, narrative, and problem-solving, offer guides to our task as teachers, and a way to see teaching and scholarship as organically related.

Teaching literature in the twenty-first century will demand more flexibility and less specialization. We can't possibly know everything about our academic field, but we can be more prepared for what we actually do in the classroom. I'd like to see an erosion of the boundaries between literary criticism and creative writing, between teaching and acting, between the abstract ethics of theory and the real ethical and moral problems involved in teaching material that raises every difficult human issue from racism to suicide. Graduate training for the PhD should include training in pedagogy, and also in acting, performance, and writing. Teachers should read contemporary literature, go to the theater and movies, watch television, write in all forms, and reflect on how all these activities contribute to what we do in class. Perhaps, then, as George Levine imagines, writing about teaching could become "as central to professional life as writing about Renaissance poetry, Derrida, Hegel, or popular culture." Perhaps as we see it as a more complex, subject-centered, and fully humanistic skill, our work of teaching could "be folded into the most serious, critical, theoretical, and scholarly thinking of the university faculty member's 'work'."[3]

I owe special thanks to the teachers of literature in the US and England who have generously answered my questions about their teaching careers: Oliver Arnold, Isobel Armstrong, Kasia Boddy, Michael Cadden, Larry Danson, John Fleming, William Gleason, Mark Hanson, Lisa Jardine, Zachary Leader, Wendy Martin, Diane Middlebrook, Jeff Nunokawa, Carol Smith, Ann Thompson, and Alex Zwerdling. My colleagues in the English Department at Princeton, where undergraduate teaching is taken very seriously, have contributed to the ideas in this book over years of meetings, lunches, and arguments in the hall. At the very beginning of my own teaching career, I met a young professor of French named English. Reader, I married him, and he has been my best pedagogical partner ever since.

As with every other subject, the best way to learn how to teach is to try to show someone else how to do it. I have worked with many talented, creative, witty, and candid graduate teaching assistants, both preceptors (discussion group leaders) in my own lecture courses, and participants in my Cotsen Seminar on Pedagogy who were assisting in a wide range of courses in the English department. I met with each group every week to discuss texts about teaching, and to talk about goals and ideas for leading discussion classes in literature. For three years, since the development of electronic discussion boards (at Princeton we use the courseware marketed by

Blackboard), we have been able to post weekly journals about how these ideas and goals actually worked in practice. The hundreds of pages of detailed commentary and correspondence we compiled would make a fascinating book in its own right; but I am very grateful that the participants have allowed me to quote passages from their postings. Most teaching descriptions I have cited anonymously, as requested, although I have identified the writer in a few places when he or she came up with an especially brilliant idea about class process.

I have never met Harold Cotsen, the Princeton alumnus who funded the seminars, but my deepest thanks to him, and to all the participants, many of them now professors and teachers of literature at other lucky universities: Sally Bachner, Karen Beckman, Laura Berol, Peter Betjemann, Lorna Brittan, Stuart Burrows, Anne Margaret Daniels, Jasmin Darznik, Wes Davis, Aileen Forbes, Denise Gigante, Marah Gubar, Adam Gussow, Kristine Haugen, Kathryn Humphreys, Anne Jamison, Howard Keeley, Paul Kelleher, Beth Machlan, Renee Mapp, Barry McCrea, Gage McWeeny, Virgil Moorefield, Jim Moyer, Dan Novak, Lev Olsen, Mika Provata, Harold Ramdass, Jessica Richard, Chris Rovee, Amada Sandoval, Stephanie Smith, Kate Stanton, Val Vinokurov, and Emily Wittman. Thanks also to the many wonderful Princeton undergraduates in my courses on Contemporary Fiction, Modern Drama, The American Short Story, and Literature of the *Fin de Siècle*, whose comments, evaluations, and weekly email postings helped me understand what was working in the classroom and what was not. Two special undergraduate research assistants, Anne Griffin and Eben Harrell, funded by the Princeton University Council on Research in the Humanities, helped me track down sources and transcribe interviews.

Teaching literature is not brain surgery. No one will die if we make a mistake about Dryden. And we can't be at our best, most reflective, most experimental every day and in every class. As Kenneth Eble writes, "teaching at the top of one's abilities is exhausting. One cannot operate at that pitch all the time and recognizing that fact is not a sign that one is falling short."[4] Some days, even some weeks or months, we may just want to be good-enough teachers, get by on knowledge and experience. Sometimes we need to fall back on the tried and true. But we can improve our students' lives and morale by sharing ideas about how to teach better, and improve our own lives and morale by thinking about why we want to teach literature in the first place. No single book can cover everything, but I hope that both beginners and veterans will find this one useful, and that my approach to the teaching of literature will be relevant for teachers in very different institutions and programs, in a wide range of national settings, and in other languages than English.

Chapter 1
The Anxiety of Teaching

Anxiety Dreams

It's the middle of the semester, and I suddenly realize that for weeks I have been skipping one of the classes I am assigned to teach. Panicked and guilt-ridden, I jump into the car, and drive frantically to the campus, but I get hopelessly lost on one-way streets, driving up and down the ramps of packed garages. Finally I park illegally, and run to the classroom building, which is on a high hill. When I arrive, breathless, to my amazement the students are still in the room, and I try to explain why I have not showed up for six weeks and to pretend that I know what we are supposed to discuss. I know that I am in trouble for this shocking dereliction of duty, and cannot explain to myself why I have been so feckless and irresponsible.

It's a teaching dream, one of the occupational hazards of all professors. My husband, who teaches French literature, has a recurring dream of "lecturing, brilliantly I feel, with unaccustomed eloquence and animation, and then I realize that I am in an L-shaped room, and that another lecturer is speaking out of sight around the corner, but to the same students I am talking to. And their rapt attentiveness is actually for that other course." Just before he retired, after 35 years of teaching, he dreamed that he was "in my old junior high school, a square building with a courtyard, with stairways at each corner. I am lost, looking in vain for my mailbox, where I will presumably find the directions to my classroom, while hordes of students rush purposefully by and bells clang ominously, signaling the start of a class I am obviously going to be late for. As I wake up in mild alarm, I wonder why I am giving my college classes in my old junior high school building, which was torn down years ago."

1

Isobel Armstrong (Birkbeck) had her most vivid teaching dream when she was at the University of Southampton. "I was giving a lecture somewhere else, on Charlotte Brontë. There was a huge audience but I felt happy and at ease. I had lots of notes. I opened the book to read a passage from the novel – and it was a totally unknown novel by Brontë I had never seen before, with themes of a green arbor, of ivy and feculent scrolls of plant work. I looked at the pages dumbfounded. What shall I do?"[1]

After many years at the University of Chicago, Wayne Booth had a dream that he had returned to Haverford, where he had started his teaching career, as Distinguished Professor of the Humanities. But he was unable to find his living quarters, or his classroom. Finally he located a catalog, and saw that he was listed to teach – in Latin. He was in panic – now it would be discovered that he was a fraud.[2]

Jane Tompkins describes her classic anxiety dream in *A Life in School*: "I'm in front of the class on the first day of school and for some reason, I'm totally unprepared . . . Throat tight, I fake a smile, grab for words, tell an anecdote, anything to hold their attention. But the strangers in rows in front of me aren't having any. They start to shuffle and murmur; they turn their heads away. The chairs scrape back, and I realize it's actually happening. The students are walking out on me."[3]

Failure, irresponsibility, panic, lack of preparation, fraudulence, disorientation are all too familiar themes of these academic versions of the gothic novel. Michael Berubé (Pennsylvania State University) has written a fascinating essay about "the psychic landscape" of teaching dreams, with their "mysterious building, spectral students, surreal classroom, sheer suffocating terror." In his own worst nightmare, "I wander into the English-department office as the semester begins to find that my course on 20th century African-American fiction, meeting later that day, has been changed to 'Avant-Garde and Representation: The Problem of the Holocaust.' I have no syllabus, nor do I know anything about the topic. Nevertheless, terrified as I am, I manage to bluff my way through the first class by asking the students for their reactions to *Schindler's List*. Thankfully, they are less annoyed by my incompetence than by the fact that the classroom has window ledges seven feet high – and no chairs."

"From what all my friends and colleagues tell me," Berubé concludes, "it doesn't matter how experienced or accomplished you are: If you care at all about your teaching, you are haunted by teaching-anxiety dreams." Why so? Because "teaching is really hard to do. If you're doing it in classes of 15 and 40 students, as I am, you're teaching in a setting where the students will find out not only what you think about x and y, but also what you are like, in some strange and intimate way. They'll get a sense of how thoroughly you

2

prepare, of course, but even more they'll see how you respond to the unexpected – to the savvy young woman who wants to know whether you're using the term 'postcolonial' in a cultural or an economic sense, to the curious junior who wonders aloud why Don DeLillo gave the name Simeon Biggs to a snappish African-American character in *Underworld*. For such moments you simply can't prepare – except by accumulating years upon years of teaching experience and weathering night upon night of anxiety dreams."[4] The fear Berubé describes is partly the fear of being outsmarted by the students; when I moved to Princeton, my husband reassured me that the brilliant student was actually the teacher's greatest ally.

Perhaps teaching literature feels especially unsettling because, unlike physicists or economists, we are not confident of our authority. Moreover, we believe that what we say in the classroom reveals the deepest aspects of ourselves. Whether we weep over Keats's letters or list his dates of publication, teaching feels like an externalization of our personality and psyche. When it works, we feel that we have succeeded; when it doesn't work, we feel that we have failed. Jane Tompkins believes that anxiety dreams are all about "the fear of failure – the failure of one's authority – and it points to the heart of what it means to be a teacher."[5] She even writes an Emily-Dickinson-like poem about the "bravery of teachers:"

> To teach is to be battered
> Scrutinized, and drained,
> Day after day. We know this.
> Still, it is never said.

"I wish I had been warned," Tompkins laments, "about what an ego-battering exercise teaching can be. Teaching, by its very nature, exposes the self to myriad forms of criticism and rejection, as well as to emulation and flattery and love. Day after day, teachers are up there, on display; no matter how good they are, it's impossible not to get shot down."[6]

Seven Types of Anxiety

Why so much angst in a profession that is outwardly so rewarding? We literature teachers have heard the familiar words of Chaucer's Clerke of Oxford – "Gladly wolde he lerne and gladly teche" – intoned at a hundred retirement dinners, and may even have declaimed them ourselves. But Chaucer's clerk did not have to face student or peer course evaluations, a ticking tenure clock, CD-ROMs, or grade inflation. Let's face it, confronting a skeptical roomful of students every morning is not always a glad pursuit. Richard Elmore, a professor at the Harvard Graduate School of Education, writes that teaching "is a messy, indeterminate, inscrutable, often intimidating, and highly uncertain task . . . Exposing one's knowledge, personality, and ego to the regular scrutiny of others in public is not easy work under the best of circumstances."[7] Even talking about our profession with any hint of idealism can bring down the sneers of the sophisticated, while it's often hard to know exactly what kind and degree of cynicism to adopt.

Moreover, literary study today is a profession simultaneously expanding intellectually and contracting economically like some Spenserian snake. So many books, so little time; so many conferences, so few jobs. The list of articles and books to master gets longer every year, and the gap between the academic star – the frequent flyer – and the academic drudge – the freeway flyer – gets wider. Those who do not have jobs feel angry; those who do feel guilty.

Anxiety dreams, I think, are about our existential sense of quest and vocation as teachers, a quest that does not get easier with age. They are scenarios that dramatize the questions we ask ourselves throughout our teaching careers: Why I am doing this with my life? Does it matter? Do I deserve to be doing it? What have I really been teaching? What have I really been learning? Where am I going? What will happen to me when I can no longer teach? These fundamental questions of identity and purpose are at the heart of literature as well, and I will try to address them throughout this book. But although the anxieties of teaching literature are deep and multiple, I will begin by looking at seven basic types of anxiety that are more immediate, professional, and concrete: lack of pedagogical training, isolation, stage fright, the conflict between teaching and publication, coverage, grading, and student or peer evaluation.

1 Lack of training

The most profound anxiety of teaching is our awareness that we are making it up as we go along. Teaching is a demanding occupation, but few of us actually have studied how to do it. Most tenured professors at the beginning of the twenty-first century picked up teaching through painful experience, doing unto others as was done unto us. Tales of initiation have a common narrative structure – how novices stumble into their first classroom, do the best they can, and gradually find ways to overcome their fears of exposure and inadequacy, and shape a teaching style that seems congenial for their own personalities and environments. Norman Maclean writes that the only advice he ever received about teaching was to "wear a different suit every day of the week." He couldn't afford that many suits, so he wore a different necktie every day instead.[8]

Jane Tompkins really opened up the question of our general lack of preparation for teaching, and our consequent anxiety about it, in a brave and groundbreaking essay for *College English* in 1990, called, with reference to the fashionable work of Paulo Freire, "Pedagogy of the Distressed." Subsequently "Pedagogy of the Distressed" led to Tompkins's influential – and controversial – book, *A Life in School: What the Teacher Learned* (1996).

Tompkins confessed that "teaching was exactly like sex for me – something you weren't supposed to talk about or focus on in any way, but that you were supposed to be able to do properly when the time came."[9] The essay generated a lot of positive letters, although the respondents also complained about Tompkins' institutional privilege, as a tenured professor at Duke. They ignored the gender connotations of her sexual metaphor, an apt parallel for women of my generation who went to college before the sexual revolution. Jane Tompkins and I had been dorm-mates at Bryn Mawr in the early 1960s. By 1990, I guess, young professors talked a lot about sexual performance, but still not much about teaching.

After Bryn Mawr, Tompkins had a Danforth Teaching Fellowship at Yale, but "nothing in that experience shed any light on what classroom teaching was about. When I asked the assistant professor I was apprenticed to for advice about the two lectures I was slated to give . . . he said 'stay close to the text.' Well, that was Yale's answer to every question about literature, and I knew it already. But as a teaching strategy, it left me groping." In her first teaching job, at Connecticut College, "my toughest course as a beginning teacher was a survey of English literature from Chaucer to Wallace Stevens. I'd never taken a survey course and had no notion of how to teach one . . . I needed to know history; I needed biographical information on the authors; I needed overarching ideas to pull the material together – everything I had been forbidden at Yale. The bottom line was I didn't have enough to say; I was always afraid I'd run out of material before the hour was up and have to stand there facing the students, my mouth opening and closing but emitting no sound."

Tompkins worried endlessly about what she was saying rather than what her students were learning. "I developed a habit of holding back on my important points, stretching out the lesser ideas and making them last until I could see I'd have enough material to get me through to the end of the period. Sometimes the main point would get lost or squeezed into the last few minutes when the students were already collecting their things, anxious about being late for the next class and no longer paying attention." Now, she reflects, "I'm amazed that my fellow Ph.D.s and I were let loose in the classrooms with virtually no preparation for what we would encounter in a human sense . . . If only I'd known, if someone I respected had talked to me honestly about teaching, I might have been saved from a lot of pain."[10]

Like Tompkins, many American professors of literature who have written about the contrast between their scholarly training and their sink-or-swim teaching started out at Yale. Alvin Kernan has reminisced about his alarming initiation into teaching under Maynard Mack in the 1950s: "Besides teaching a small discussion session, each of us had to take turns delivering the weekly lectures on the great works of Western literature. Maynard set the pace – he crafted his lectures as tightly as a poem while keeping his words direct and plain – but when we lectured he sat in the audience conspicuously and busily writing in a large notebook. So long as he wrote, you were OK, but when he looked up, paused, and then closed the notebook you had ceased to interest him, and since he was the most powerful professor in the humanities, it meant your Yale career was over. Everything rode on those Tuesday lectures, and because we had almost no experience at lecturing, the learning curve was very steep."[11]

As an aspiring young black scholar, Houston Baker (Pennsylvania) had learned in graduate school at Yale in the 1970s "how to write critical prose and how to carry myself with professional decorum and collegial good taste. I had not actively prepared myself to teach, however, for I assumed that teaching was merely a technical delivery system for critical knowledge. I thought of the activity as the last relay in the academic olympiad – the final transfer of the fire of the gods by the newly minted Ph.D." Baker was shocked when a student at Yale came to the office to tell him that the class was in mutiny: "Those spirit-of-the-age lectures are driving us crazy." It was much later that he incorporated his own African-American identity into the classroom and into his teaching style.[12]

Michael Cadden, the head of the theater and dance program at Princeton, and a winner of the university's distinguished teaching award, had no pedagogical training at all as a Yale graduate student in the drama school. He was hired to teach in a freshman course in the interdisciplinary honors program, covering the Bible to Beckett. Cadden had no trouble with the discussion part of teaching, where his acting experience and outgoing personality stood him in good stead; but it took him a long time to discover a lecture mode. He wanted to emulate Yale professor Alvin Kernan, who made Shakespeare's characters "sound like friends of his"; and he began with the nervous impulse to write everything out. Cadden endured many an all-nighter. Then his friend Suzanne Wofford suggested that the method wasn't working for him; he was too stiff and tied down to his script. Cadden tried writing the lecture out, but not reading it, and then gradually moved by stages to using only notes.[13]

Alex Zwerdling (Berkeley) had been a graduate student at Princeton, where one memorable professor "knew none of the students even by the sixth week of the term. The only problems he could take seriously were ones that had already been defined. He lectured to the seminar from yellowing cards without looking up. Once a card literally crumbled in his hands." Zwerdling's first job at Swarthmore, and his first teaching assignment, was a course on the gothic novel. He was "very unprepared. I lectured the first day and said everything I knew. I had zero sense of audience."[14]

In Britain too, lack of preparation was the norm. Isobel Armstrong "always thought I could do it better than those who taught me at Leicester." But before her first lecture at University College London on *Wuthering Heights*, she was "shaking with terror." For three years, she was unable to sleep the night before a lecture. Lisa Jardine (Queen Mary College) had no training, but changed her teaching dramatically in 1989 after she was sent on a week-long course for broadcasters and "taught how to ask good questions," and also after she saw Isobel Armstrong conduct a graduate seminar, using small groups and dialog.[15]

Coppelia Kahn had been a graduate student at Berkeley. When she started teaching at Wesleyan, "my teaching was a disaster. I was assigned the first half (Chaucer to Dryden) of the required majors' survey . . . I treated the undergraduates like graduate students, assuming they already understood concepts like period, convention, genre, lecturing them to death and allowing no time for discussion. They rebelled, and I landed in therapy."[16]

The pedagogy of the depressed described by Kahn and others is still all too frequent. Despite recent efforts to improve the training of college teachers, especially in Britain, the myths of the "born teacher" and the mystique of good teaching as the natural complement of scholarly research still undermine departmental commitments to preparing graduate students for teaching careers.

Someday soon, I hope, teaching preparation will be a requirement; meanwhile, every teacher of literature should have a personal collection of well-thumbed pedagogy guidebooks, which provide an overview of research on learning in higher education, plus theories, and techniques for course design, lecturing, leading discussions, giving examinations, grading, dealing with problem students, counseling, advising, and handling cheating or plagiarism. You may have to order them; until a few years back, they were certainly not in my university bookstore or library. Many publishers of educational guidebooks, such as Jossey-Bass and Kogan Page, don't even advertise or exhibit at the MLA, which ought to tell us something about the current state of the profession. Keep your eyes open for ads and reviews in places like the *Chronicle of Higher Education, Times Higher Education Supplement, College English*, and the many websites now available through university teaching centers. If you have such a center on your campus, it will have a library of these books. I think every department should have one too, and keep it updated.

My top pick for a general handbook is Wilbert J. McKeachie's *Teaching Tips: Strategies, Research, and Theory for College and University Teachers*, from Houghton Mifflin. McKeachie, at the University of Michigan, is one of the pioneers of the active learning movement in higher education; the tenth edition of *Teaching Tips* also includes sections by other academics from The Open University, Ohio State, and the University of Texas. McKeachie keeps in touch with colleagues outside the United States who are interested in improving teaching, so his advice is not culture-bound. *Teaching Tips* is appropriate for all disciplines and fields, for experienced teachers as well as beginners. Literature professors will find the sections of the book on ethics and higher-level goals such as motivation, thinking, and values especially provocative.

A second book I have found useful is John Biggs, *Teaching for Quality Learning at University*. Biggs has taught at universities in Australia, Canada, and Hong Kong, and now teaches at the University of New South Wales, so he brings a more international perspective than McKeachie's American one. He has an excellent chapter on teaching international students. Biggs emphasizes reflection, and sets out a framework to look at teaching reflectively. He believes that there is no single ideal way to teach; what matters is "how we *conceive* the process of teaching, and through reflection come to some conclusion about how we may do our particular job better."[17]

The third book I have found essential – alas, now out of print – is Kenneth J. Eble's *The Craft of Teaching*. Eble was a professor of English at the University of Utah who died in 1988. From 1969 to 1971, he directed the Project to Improve College Teaching, co-sponsored by the Association of American University Professors (AAUP) and Association of American Colleges (AAC) and funded by the Carnegie Corporation. Eble is a realist and an optimist, the kind of teaching guru you want to consult at 3 a.m. when the prospect of tomorrow's class seems hopeless. He insists that teaching is a skill that can be learned; and that we need to keep "a sense of play in teaching . . . teaching is an improviser's art."[18]

In addition, there is a great deal of information scattered around about what teachers of literature actually do. The Modern Language Association series on approaches to teaching world literature now numbers over 70

volumes. In the earlier volumes, the essays are often more about critical interpretation than actual teaching, but the more recent collections offer hands-
on advice. I have cited many of those essays here, as well as others in the
new journal *Pedagogy*, and in various scholarly journals from *Shakespeare
Quarterly* to *Eighteenth-Century Studies* and *College English* that have published imaginative articles on teaching specific writers, genres, periods, and
texts. The *Chronicle of Higher Education* and the *Times Higher Education
Supplement* both publish personal accounts of teaching practice. In England,
the English Subject Centre at Royal Holloway College publishes a newsletter three times a year and maintains a website (www.rhul.ac.uk/ltsn/
english/). Articles in the *ADE Bulletin*, the publication of the MLA for
English department chairs, frequently address teaching experience. The
millennium issue of PMLA, which came out in December 2000, is a rich
compilation of information about the way teaching literature has changed
over the past century.

2 Isolation

One of the best aspects of the work of teaching is that, unlike scholarship,
it does not have to be original to be good. We can borrow ideas and methods
from our colleagues and our predecessors, dead or alive; we can imitate, copy,
and plunder in the confidence that our students will benefit from every good
teaching technique we can put into action in our own classroom. Moreover,
as teachers, we are not in competition with each other. Teaching is not a
zero-sum game, with the success of one subtracting from the success of
another; and indeed an effective, inspiring introductory or survey course in
a department will only generate more students interested in advanced
courses.

But it is not always easy to find out what our colleagues are doing behind
those closed classroom doors. Ironically, according to Parker J. Palmer,
"Teaching is perhaps the most privatized of all the public professions.
Though we teach in front of students, we almost always teach solo, out of
collegial sight – as contrasted with surgeons or lawyers, who work in the
presence of others who know their craft well . . . When we walk into our
workplace, the classroom, we close the door on our colleagues. When we
emerge, we rarely talk about what happened or what needs to happen next,
for we have no shared experience to talk about."[19]

Some of that privatization is now breaking down in the United States
because of widespread use of the internet to circulate syllabi and to publish
student course evaluations. In the UK, since the Dearing Report of 1997,
centralized (and much hated) teaching assessment requirements instituted

by the Labour government and the Institute for Learning and Teaching (ILT) have made teaching in higher education very public, at the cost of a great deal of bureaucracy and regimentation. But despite the mockery with which teachers of literature in Britain greet the materials on pedagogy with which they are deluged, the conversation about teaching has clearly changed for the better. In many British universities, beginning faculty participate in a term of workshops with other new teachers. The anxieties of isolation seem to be on the decline.

I was blessed as a beginning assistant professor to be in a department at Douglass College where my colleagues, under the energetic leadership of Barrett Mandel – a pioneer in the development of literary pedagogy – met regularly to discuss teaching approaches and theories. I've also been able to team-teach regularly, and to share ideas and problems with imaginative friends. But I think that the best immediate solution to feelings of isolation is to redefine the experience of listening to conference papers and professional lectures as one of learning. If classroom teaching is private and isolated, lecturing is a public display of pedagogical techniques or their absence. It is a regular opportunity for literature teachers to renew our own student roles, and to reflect on how we respond to various teaching styles.

Moreover, when it takes place outside the classroom in the form of lecturing, we live very comfortably with the necessity of being heard and watched by our colleagues and peers. This paradox is so because we have defined lecturing and giving papers in ways that obscure or occlude their pedagogical elements. On one side, we issue heartfelt calls for greater openness and a wider conversation about teaching, as Palmer notes: "There is only one honest way to evaluate the many varieties of good teaching with the subtlety required: it is called being there. We must observe each other teach, at least occasionally – and we must spend more time talking to each other about teaching."[20] On the other side, we spend ever-expanding amounts of time giving and listening to job talks, conference papers, and invited lectures and colloquia, and ignore the opportunity they provide for seeing other people teach, for observing techniques as well as tics, and for talking about the teaching role as part of the professional career.

Certainly listening to professional academic lectures has had the most influence, both positive and negative, on my own teaching practice of anything else I have learned about it. Sander Gilman (Illinois at Chicago) makes every lecture a dialog with his audience. Oxford's Gillian Beer generates compelling enthusiasm and intellectual involvement. Hazel Carby (Yale) was the first person I ever saw using video clips in a public lecture. As audiences, we often waste these occasions, letting our minds wander, applauding politely, asking phony or competitive questions, and finding ways to steer the conversation around to our own specialties and interests. It's as stylized a routine as a Victorian afternoon call. If only we could leave our cards, with the corners folded down, instead of having to sit through these rituals, we would have more time to plan our own courses. Listening to Stanley Fish, during a summer at the School for Criticism and Theory, ask lecturers questions that were tough, direct, and shockingly honest gave me the courage to ask some real questions myself, and to think much harder about the responses I wanted from my students. I learned a lot about teaching from those sessions.

But we could use bad lecturers as well as great ones to initiate a public conversation about teaching, and to put those weary hours of Sitzfleisch to some intellectual use. If we care about teaching, the public lecture should be our laboratory, and not just our duty.

3 Teaching versus research

"I have professors telling me," one graduate student laments, " 'Spend as little time as possible on your teaching, and make sure you're a good researcher.' "[21] For decades, professors of literature have discussed the conflicts between teaching and scholarly publication. Marjorie Hope Nicolson, the president of the MLA in 1963, noted that although those at the MLA annual meeting called themselves scholars, "all of us are also teachers, who earn our bread by teaching rather than scholarship – which is fortunate, since we would not eat the driest bread if we were dependent merely upon the latter."[22] On the other hand, as George Levine points out, in a larger sense faculty do indeed earn their bread by scholarship: "While teaching literature is what faculty get hired to do, it would be merely disingenuous to argue that teaching literature – at least at major research universities – is not the primary focus of faculty attention or what most faculty get rewarded for doing or writing about."[23] We call teaching our jobs, but we call our research our work. And the two conflict for our attention and our time.

Gerald Graff, who has written widely about education and the professing of literature, argues that we can't overcome the gap by simply mandating that teaching should count as much as scholarship. His suggestion is that we should reconceive our "research in ways that make it more teachable."[24] I believe the opposite: that we should reconceive our pedagogy to make it as intellectually challenging as our research. What we need, in the words of Diana Laurillard of Britain's Open University, is "to find an infrastructure that enables university teachers to be as professional in their teaching as they aspire to be in their research."[25] For literature teachers, that means reflecting upon the relationship between what we teach and how we teach

11

it, in new ways, so that the same problems we deal with in our research, including performance and narrative, become part of our pedagogical vocabulary.

Of course, this will have its anxieties too, as teaching becomes another subject of our research and publication. As Wayne Booth ruefully writes in his teaching journal, "the chief obstacle to my teaching *at the moment* is my half-baked plan for a book about teaching."[26]

4 Coverage

As Booth wryly suggests, attending to the classroom is always in competition with other parts of our job. The sheer quantity of literary publication, both primary and secondary, is more daunting every year. Keeping up is hard to do, whether you are a medievalist or a postmodernist. In my area of specialization, contemporary fiction, there's a whole new truckload of novels and stories to read every fall, not to mention the reviews and the interviews and all the latest theoretical twists and turns from Armstrong to Zizek.

Our internalized anxieties about the infinite amount of literary knowledge and the finite amount of academic time come together in worries about course coverage. How much do students need to know in order to gain real understanding of the complexities of any literary text or author, let alone a historical period? As Stephen Greenblatt (Harvard) observes, literature in English is characterized by "spectacular abundance," as is "the media through which students can encounter and explore that literature." Even Greenblatt confesses that "abundance wonderfully complicates the job of syllabus writing" and he himself "nearly tore [his] hair out trying to fit everything in" to his course.[27]

One desperate professorial solution to abundance is to assign as much as humanly possible. I've frequently been guilty of what Kathy Overhulse Smith (Indiana) calls "the mistaken notion that mere exposure to particular ideas, texts, or authors will effect student learning. How many times, during a rushed semester, have we caught ourselves thinking, 'Well, even if we don't have time to cover this [author, text, idea] in class today, I have at least assigned it and can therefore be satisfied that my students have been at least exposed to it.' Such thinking may enable us momentarily to assure ourselves that we have our done our duty and thereby covered our professional behinds, but the distress we experience later on discovering how little an impression the author, text, or idea made on our students proves how superficial our rationalization was."[28]

The advent of the internet and CD-ROMs, and the age of new anthologies, makes the problem of coverage more intellectually perplexing, even if it is mechanically more efficient – perhaps *because* it is mechanically more efficient. The seventh edition of *The Norton Anthology of English Literature*, edited by Greenblatt among others, now comes with an online archive and a CD. With these added materials, Greenblatt explains, the teacher's problems of "textual triage" are greatly relieved. Every text that was cut from the anthology, or shortened, in order to make room for the ever-expanding canon of literary works, is in the Norton Online Archive, along with a Topics section containing 1,000 illustrations and 250 "explorations designed to stimulate critical thinking and generate paper topics."[29]

But what this richness means for the teacher is an even greater pressure to cover everything. We can no longer offer our old standby excuses of textual unavailability or expense, and our traditional assumption – that first-rate teaching is primarily about content, and the quantity of content, rather than process, and the quality of process – is harder to resist. Yet obsession with coverage and content is one of the main barriers to good teaching. According to Paul Ramsden, "we should rather strive to include less . . . Resisting the temptation to add more and more content is extremely difficult if a lecturer sees undergraduate student learning as an obstacle course or as a process of acquiring huge quantities of information . . . Some lecturers seem to think this approach has the effect of a kind of perverted commando training course, sharpening the powers of the strong and eliminating the weak."[30]

One of the most difficult tasks for a literature teacher is deciding what to leave out. Instead of aiming for comprehensive coverage, we have to think about what students need to read in order to establish a basis for further learning, and we have to adjust our intellectual aspirations to a realistic workload.

5 Performance

Having struggled with textual triage, with deciding what is essential to teach undergraduates and what is inessential, we have to face the reality of standing up in front of a group to teach, and its symptoms of stage fright and performance anxiety. One professor recalls that "in the early years of teaching, my anxiety level rose as the time to walk into class approached. My breathing was quick and shallow, and often a headache accompanied me through the door. I felt the terrifying responsibility of maintaining control over myself, my words, my body, and, not least, the class . . . It took voice lessons and a Gestalt course in group process to bring myself back into my body."[31] An Oxford don needed a shot of brandy before he could face his class; medievalist Richard Fraher says "even old stagers in the academic pro-

13

fession have been known to confess that their hearts pound painfully before each lecture; some have nightmares that the clock hands are moving backwards while they speak, or that they look up to find an empty hall."[32] As Wayne Booth wonders, "how can anyone claim 'to love teaching' if he feels such relief when it's *over and done?*"[33]

Teaching the Literature of the *Fin de Siècle* at Princeton in the late 1980s, I suddenly developed a case of nerves and had to steel myself each week to walk into the classroom I had been assigned – the astronomy lecture hall, a round windowless room, like the inside of a cave. I was teaching about decadence, degeneration, colonialism, and homoeroticism in writers of the 1880s and 1890s, including Kipling, Stevenson, Haggard, Stoker, and Conrad, and of course Freud. In the back row of the auditorium sat a group of tall male students, with a body language of extreme resistance and hostility – folded arms, stony faces, occasional snickers and whispers. (Indeed, one of these students has gone on to become the editor of the men's magazine *Maxim*, and he recently told the Princeton alumni magazine that he still wants to prove that I am wrong about women in slasher films.) As the semester went on, I became increasingly anxious about lecturing, even afraid of losing my voice.

Was it performance anxiety? About halfway through the term, an actor friend recommended that I read a book on stage fright, which interpreted some of the psychoanalytic aspects of performing as oral anxieties. Appearing before an audience is in some sense being nurtured and fed by them – fed by their attention, their applause, their love. But performance is also an experience of being fed *to* them, being devoured and consumed. For this reason, actors or comedians have ritual metaphors about killing or slaying the audience, knocking them dead. Ironically, one of the texts that engendered the most hostile activity from the back row was Freud's "Medusa's Head," that brief allegory of castration fears and the apotropaic act of displaying the Medusa symbol to intimidate the Evil Spirit. And I realized that the classroom I taught in felt like a mouth.

In contrast to the lecture, the weekly discussion section, to which I always brought cookies, was going very well. Bringing the cookies to my discussion group was my apotropaic gesture, a surrogate offering. What I meant by it was "Eat these and leave me alone." I understood that I was conflicted about being the Medusa-like authority figure who confronted students with such controversial and threatening material, and the nurturer who had played more conventional and maternal roles in the classroom. I stopped bringing the cookies, tried to confront the issues of dissent in lecture and precept, and my stage fright went away.

14

But I now believe that performance anxiety relates to the ways faculty project their own fears onto their students, just as students project their fears onto professors. In this course, I myself turned the students in the back row into what Parker Palmer calls the generic Students from Hell. According to Palmer, anxiety about the Student from Hell comes from two sources – the "need to be popular with young people," which he regards as pathological; and the "need to be in life-giving communion with the young," "to stay connected with the life of the rising generation," which he sees as part of the generativity that enables us to stay genuine and engaged.[34]

If I had been able to get to know these students individually, the class would have felt much more comfortable to me, but I was new to Princeton and still nervous about challenging its separation of lecture and precept. In my precept, what saved me was not the cookies, but the personal contact with students. They were not intimidating strangers, but people I knew, and who knew me.

In addition to anxiety about performing, many teachers feel anxiety about the very idea of performance, which strikes them as cheap, hammy, and anti-intellectual. Frank Kermode memorably describes one performative don, D. J. Gordon at Liverpool: "From his gait on entry to his last word, all was theatre . . . He would begin by describing the occasion of the masque or entertainment, or the sterling character, unaccountably neglected by all previous commentators, of some work of art . . . The opening passage of the lecture would contain some thrilling disclosure that opened up a new vista on history, some moment in the narrative that would turn out to be critical . . . The lecturer would require many slides, always projected on two screens . . . The gesticulations, the rehearsed pauses, the refined sneer or downward glance of contempt that companied allusions to other workers in the field, the little *moues* of self-satisfaction, all these combined to make his lectures as good as a play; not a mere farce because he was usually saying something new and interesting, and, after all, saying it memorably."[35] Despite the concession in that last phrase, Kermode's distaste for what he sees as a narcissistic mode is clear.

For Jane Tompkins, who writes about herself instead of her colleagues, classroom "performance" is simply naked ego and showing off – everything she deplores in academia. Her epiphany as a teacher came, she writes, when she suddenly realized that while "for my entire teaching life I had always thought that what I was doing was helping my students to understand the material we were studying . . . what I had actually been concerned with was showing the students how smart I was, how knowledgeable I was, and how well prepared I was for class. I had been putting on a performance whose true goal was not to help the students learn, as I had thought, but to perform before them in such a way that they would have a good opinion of me."[36]

Patricia Hampl is another teacher with second thoughts about her own performance as addictive. "My teaching was operatic," she confesses. "Or maybe it wasn't an aria with improbable high notes, but a jazz improvisation built of riffs I seemed to maneuver successfully to the delight of my indulgent audience. I remade myself as an unlikely amalgam of the earnest and the hip . . . It felt like a radiance, not a force, and I never doubted it was benign." But after taking ten years off to write poetry and fiction, Hampl returned to the classroom in a different spirit. "My diva self had stayed back there in the 1960s past . . . I didn't have the will to perform. I had no pirouettes left in me. I didn't want teaching to be a high . . . I knew I would not – could not – sustain that kind of performance again. It was like knowing I'd never do cocaine again."[37]

In an essay on education that appeared in *Harper's*, Mark Edmundson (University of Virginia), laments the students' expectations that he will perform on the podium, and rejects his popularity in course evaluations as false praise: "I'm disturbed by the serene belief that my function – and, more important, Freud's, or Shakespeare's, or Blake's – is to divert, entertain, and interest. Observes one respondent, not at all unrepresentative: 'Edmundson has done a fantastic job of presenting this difficult, important & controversial material in an enjoyable and approachable way.' Thanks but no thanks. I don't teach to amuse, divert, or even, for that matter, to be merely interesting . . . but the affability and the one-liners often seem to be all that land with the students." Methinks that Edmundson protests too much, especially when he goes on to complain that his students find him "urbane . . . generous, funny, and loose."[38] The poor guy. Yet in the zero-sum games of academe, it's true that being likable and funny seems to cancel out rigor and intelligence.

On the other hand, being dull rather than entertaining is no guarantee of intellectual distinction either. We have a professional contempt for any kind of teaching that seems phony, flashy, or showy. But, as Kenneth Eble comments, "in my observation of teachers on many campuses over the past decade, I have seen fewer charlatans than mediocrities and been less appalled by flashy deception than by undisguised dullness. And I have never encountered any evidence that a dull and stodgy presentation necessarily carries with it an extra measure of truth and virtue." Performance, and speaking to strangers, Eble points out, is part of the job; but without courting media popularity, teachers can "learn from the performing arts." It should be part of a teacher's training to "develop a speaking voice that has range, force, and direction; a presence that uses the dynamics of physical movement to lend conviction to inner strengths of mind and imagination; and the dramatic abilities that can fashion scenes, build climaxes, manage stage props and business."[39]

Larry Danson, who teaches Shakespeare and other drama courses at Princeton, found ways to overcome his performance anxiety early in his career as a lecturer. Danson now can understand the process by which he became a confident lecturer: "I had to re-evaluate my own feelings and interpret nervousness as eagerness. I think that sometimes what you interpret as fear is actually a terrific desire to do well, and young teachers have to learn to manage that desire and make that nervous energy an ally rather than an enemy." He believes that "the secret of public speaking is not to give in to secondary anxiety – I'm scared, and I'm scared of being scared. Of course you are scared of going into a classroom and performing in public. Who isn't? But that's where your energy will come from. Reinterpret your reluctance to perform as a desire to perform. Your reluctance to make a fool out of yourself in front of your students is in fact a desire to perform for them." Danson also reflects eloquently on the secret fears of being judged, making mistakes, and being found wanting common to all teachers. "I think you have to get over the feeling that the students are your judges. But remember they don't want you to hold back. Sometimes beginning teachers are afraid – what would happen if I let myself go? If I spoke on my feet? We're scared of being found out, so we stop communicating. But you do want to be found out, because inevitably you do know more than these students, you do have something to say. Being in the now, present, at this moment, thinking out loud, rather than being bound to overwhelming notes, is absolutely essential. And when you entertain the students and engage the students and see that happening, you'll realize, 'Well, letting go isn't something I need to be afraid of; it's actually what I have to let happen.' "[40]

6 Grading

Grading produces anxiety for teachers as well as for students. Indeed, I often tell myself that grading is the part of the job I get paid for (Booth calls it "the detested task") while the rest of teaching is something I would do for free.[41]

In the past few years, anxieties have increased as charges of "grade inflation" have made headlines not only in professional publications but also in the media at large. In the fall of 2001, when Harvard president Lawrence Summers reprimanded professor Cornel West for the alleged grade inflation in his undergraduate course in African-American studies – the second-largest course at the university – the reverberations were heard from Los Angeles to London. Accusations of grade inflation at Harvard (where half the grades are now either A– or A), and elsewhere, have been perennial for decades; they had been raised in April 2001 by conservative Harvey Mansfield, a professor of government at Harvard. Mansfield charged that high grades were the result of faculty flattering students' "self-esteem" to gain "fleeting popularity," and were a sign that faculty had become cynical about their teaching. They had begun, he argues, in the late 1960s, when "white professors, imbibing the spirit of affirmative action, stopped giving low or average grades to black students and, to justify or conceal it, stopped giving those grades to white students as well."

A notable omission in the angry and nasty exchanges about grade inflation at Harvard – and the more polite and subdued, but equally concerned exchanges about grade inflation elsewhere – was any discussion of the relationship of grades to learning and the learning process. Mansfield takes it as self-evident that any teacher would want "to discriminate the best from the very good," and so on.[42] But virtually all specialists in higher education, while they acknowledge that assessment is part of the system and that we must devise fair, consistent, and accurate ways of assessing learning, are critical of grades as such, and particularly of grading on a curve.

I wonder how much deans, university presidents, and boards of trustees know that the consistent theme in the best pedagogical writing is, as Wilbert McKeachie – probably the most influential and internationally-used expert on university teaching – declares about assessment, *"assigning grades is not the most important function"* (my italics).[43] Assessment is about helping students learn – not about sorting them out for employers, punishing them, or showing how tough you are.

In *Mastering the Techniques of Teaching*, Joseph Lowman notes that "colleges, academic departments, or instructors who infer that their students learn more because average grades are lower delude themselves." The "quality of a college education is more a function of the faculty, the teaching, and the overall student population than of grading stringency." Further, for "most students and many college teachers, tests and grades are an unpleasant and unavoidable reality." Some teachers actively dread grading; others deeply enjoy it. But "for everyone personally associated with higher education – students, faculty, and parents – evaluation is an emotionally charged topic."[44] The first paper or exam of the course is certainly a shock for the teacher. The honeymoon is over; these smiling, enthusiastic young people who seem so interested in the literature turn out to be incapable of getting the characters' names right or writing a coherent paragraph. Indeed, Lowman explains, "the first set of exam papers of a term is particularly emotional, reminding instructor and students of the evaluative aspect of their

18

relationship. Novice teachers' first sets of papers can be particularly disheartening and can lead them to question both their competence and their motivation for an academic career."[45]

Despite all these anxieties, teachers can learn how to plan assignments and construct tests that match objectives to evaluation, and find ways to challenge students without giving in to ill-informed administrative pressure to fight "grade inflation" without concern for learning and teaching. In my view, the real problem is why all the students at Harvard do not get A grades. If these brilliant and intellectually eager undergraduates cannot be motivated and taught by their faculty to master the course material, perhaps we should ask why.

7 Evaluation

Reading student teaching evaluations, professors feel that we have been judged as human beings. I have seen colleagues in tears over these bi-annual comments, and I myself can remember every negative one I've ever received, back to the first round at the University of California at Davis when I was a TA: "Worst part of the course: those ugly pins on those nice dresses." In retrospect, I know the student referred to my peace buttons; then I thought he meant my legs. Public exposure is even worse, and we do not like others to examine too closely the interaction that takes place in a classroom between ourselves and our students. At Princeton in the 1960s, one professor wanted to bring his psychotherapist to his seminar to analyze the dynamics of the group; the administration refused the request, to the faculty's huge relief.

Many teachers are defensively suspicious of teaching evaluations, and dismiss them as nothing more than popularity contests. One of the most persistent myths in academe is that the harsh and unpleasant, or mumbling and droning professor who never does well on evaluations is in fact the one students will remember and cherish in years to come. Wayne Booth affectionately recalls George Williamson, who would "come into the classroom and shuffle, shifty-eyed, to a little platform, open an attaché case in front of him in such a way as to prevent all eye contact, focus his eyes alternately on the text and a far high corner of the room, and proceed to explicate T. S. Eliot's poems." Surprise, surprise – Booth soon realizes that he is "learning a lot, far more than I had learned in many a more engaging class."[46]

All very well; but what about the other students in that room? Teaching is mysterious, and when students are interested in the material, they will learn under any circumstances. But the tough drill-sergeant teacher, or the talking-to-himself teacher is not a model to emulate. Unless we are confident that among our students sits a young Wayne Booth, we are much better off using student evaluations as guides to improvement. Isobel Armstrong encountered student teaching evaluations for the first time when she was a visiting professor at Princeton. "They gave me a low rating on encouraging student participation. I was startled but completely transformed; since then I've made sure that everyone in the class says something. Learning their names is the key."

With that end in mind, we should supplement the standard university forms, administered at the end of the term, and which are judgmental rather than useful, like final grades, with informal but confidential mid-semester evaluations we prepare and distribute ourselves. The feedback from these evaluations can be used to make quick adjustments, and simply to ask the students early on to tell you what they think is a step towards improved communication.

Up from Anxiety

Of course, these seven types of anxiety overlap and even occur simultaneously. Some teachers feel that their luck is so bad that anxiety determines most of their experience in the classroom. "Teaching is never boring," Wayne Booth concludes, "but it is a profession that can seem, on a bad day, after a bad class, quite simply intolerable."[47]

But even if you enjoy yourself as a teacher and have very few bad days or nights, you can avoid the occasional bout of anxiety by overcoming the isolation of teaching – finding out what other teachers do, reflecting on the ways that literature as a subject contains its own pedagogical schema, discussing the challenges of teaching in difficult times, and the methods of teaching dangerous issues. Despite its anxieties, teaching literature offers us the best of all subjects to teach. As one MLA president said in 1942, "We hold in our hands the best cards in the scholastic pack, we are rich in trumps, and if we haven't sense enough to play them, we shall have no one but ourselves to blame."[48] None of us can teach all of the students all of the time. But for those occasions when we are ready to tackle the anxieties of teaching, and go for the grand slam, this book is a guide to playing our trumps.

Chapter 2
Theories
of Teaching
Literature

Definitions: What is Literature?

Do we have to define literature before we can teach it? George Levine thinks so; he writes that "teaching literature . . . requires a clear idea of what literature is . . . It requires, in fact, some very self-conscious theorizing."[1]

But I disagree. That self-conscious theorizing usually means entering a long dark tunnel from which few teachers, let alone clear ideas about literature, emerge. These days, you need the chutzpah of a Terry Eagleton to have a stab at defining "literature" at all, and even he concedes that "anything can be literature, and . . . any belief that the study of literature is the study of a stable, well-definable entity, as entomology is the study of insects, can be abandoned as a chimera. Some kinds of fiction are literature and some are not; some literature is fictional and some is not; some literature is verbally self-regarding, while some highly-wrought rhetoric is not literature. Literature, in the sense of a set of works of assured and unalterable value, distinguished by certain shared, inherent properties, does not exist." On the other hand, Eagleton admits, literature often uses a heightened and excessive language. "If you approach me at a bus stop," he quips, "and murmur 'Thou still unravished bride of quietness,' then I know I am in the presence of the literary."[2]

Of course, if your bus stop is not in Oxford, and if you are not a teacher of literature, the Keatsian murmurings that alert Terry Eagleton to the presence of the literary may well alert you to the presence of a nut-case. Eagleton is taking a satiric and oblique approach to defining literature, but unfortunately, many teachers continue to wrestle endlessly with the impossible task of definition, and to twist themselves into semantic knots.

I am going to cut through these knots and tangles. Realistically speaking, literature, as Roland Barthes said, is "what gets taught." And what gets taught ranges from the classics, the canon, the great tradition of English and American works; to postcolonial literature in English from all over the world; to popular literature, including best-sellers. For my purposes in this book, teaching literature means teaching fiction, poems, plays, or critical essays, whether by Wordsworth or Maya Angelou, Matthew Arnold or Homi Bhabha, Jane Austen or Stephen King, Shakespeare or David Hare. English professors also teach film, television, and all kinds of cultural materials that fall outside these literary rubrics, and I am not meaning to suggest that they are illegitimate; but for those areas there are already special manuals of teaching and analysis. Moreover, while teachers of literature now claim the rights of access to many kinds of cultural texts, we still retain our pride of expertise with regard to fiction, poems, and plays.

Goals: Why Teach Literature?

If we can't agree on a definition of literature, can we agree on the goals of teaching literary texts? Probably not. In the past, most educators agreed that teaching literature was a way of making people better human beings and better citizens. When English literature became a course of study at University College London in the 1820s, its purpose was to moralize, civilize, and humanize. In the United States, after the Civil War, literature was viewed as a "repository of moral and spiritual values," bestowing a sense too of a national culture and heritage.[3] To Yale's William Lyon Phelps, at the beginning of the twentieth century, "teaching was preaching" about Christian values and moral uplift.[4] Classical and modern literature was regarded as a quasi-religious repository of spiritual guidance.

In Oxbridge at the beginning of the twentieth century, however, English literature had become the academic province of dilettantes and gentlemanly aesthetes. To F. R. Leavis, at Cambridge in the 1930s, the serious study of English literature, the great tradition, was instead the chief weapon against the corruption and vulgarity of mass urban industrial society. As Eagleton writes in *Literary Theory*, "in the early 1920s it was desperately unclear why English was worth studying at all; by the early 1930s it had become a question of why it was worth wasting your time on anything else. English was not only a subject worth studying, but *the* supremely civilizing pursuit . . . English was an arena in which the most fundamental questions of human

existence – what it meant to be a person, to engage in significant relationship with others, to live from the vital center of the most essential values –
were thrown into vivid relief and made the object of the most intensive
scrutiny."[5]

Some of these goals are still latent in literary study, although we no longer
want to make them explicit. "There is no more need to be a card-carrying
Leavisite today," Eagleton observes, "than there is to be a card-carrying
Copernican: that current has entered the bloodstream of English studies in
England as Copernicus reshaped our astronomical beliefs."[6] In the United
States, the objectivity and formalism of the New Critics in the 1940s and
50s was both similar to Leavis's scrutiny and I. A. Richard's practical criticism of literary texts, but much more conservatively cut off from social analysis and protest. New Critical close reading isolated the text from historical
contexts and subjective interpretation, and offered a tough-minded quasi-
scientific methodology that gave literary study some parity with the sciences
as an academic discipline. The poem, the favored pedagogical genre of the
New Criticism, was a language laboratory of irony, tone, paradox, tension,
and symbolism, But it was also an aesthetic sanctuary and harmonious retreat
from social conflict. Therefore, to Marxist critics like Eagleton, the New
Criticism was "a recipe for political inertia, and thus for submission to the
political status quo."[7]

During the 1960s and 1970s, teaching literature became an explicitly
political act for radical and minority groups in the university. English departments were the places where feminist and African-American critics first began
to initiate courses and put pressure on the curriculum to include black and
women writers. Their efforts heralded a paradigm shift in canon formation
and literary studies generally, and a repudiation of formalism in favor of a
more engaged and partisan reading that saw the goal of literary study as the
formation of personal identity and political struggle. In African-American
studies, Frances Smith Foster recalls, "in the 1960s most classes began with
mimetic inquiry. Is the book 'telling the truth'? Is this poet 'for' or 'against'
the struggle? What does this play say about 'us' and 'them'?"[8] Women's
studies courses turned to literature for enlightenment about the female
psyche and the roots of sexual oppression. Literature was a mode of
consciousness-raising, or awakening, for feminist anger and protest.

But the theory revolution of the 1970s quickly shifted attention away
from the mimetic use of literature. Indeed, teaching literature became a
branch of philosophical inquiry about signification, representation, aporia,
and ideology. By the 1980s, symposia on the teaching of literature were
embattled over the importance of theory, and what many saw as the substi-
tution of secondary critical and theoretical texts over imaginative literature

23

itself. In 1988, in *Teaching Literature: What is Needed Now*, a number of English professors offered conflicting views on literary goals, from Helen Vendler arguing that we should teach students to love what we have loved – meaning works of the imagination – to J. Hillis Miller declaring that "all reading and teaching of literature is theoretical."[9] Neither extreme works as a goal for teaching. What if a teacher of literature happens to love Derrida a lot more than Dickens (not by any means a hypothetical proposition these days)? And what happens to the pure pleasure of primary reading, and the open-endedness of teaching if theory is the central value?

At some level, whether we believe in pleasure, politics, or philosophy as the goal, all of us who teach literature believe that it is important not only in education but in life. Other long-time teachers of literature have testified to the joy their work has brought to their lives, and their faith in its future. Leslie Fiedler expresses his belief in "English for everyone – an introduction to works of the imagination over which all humankind can weep, laugh, shudder, and be titillated; communal dreams, shared hallucinations – which in a time when everything else tends to divide us from each other, join us together, men and women, adults and children, educated and uneducated, black and white, yellow and brown – even, perhaps, teachers and students."[10]

Among the more abstract sources of our present anxieties is our inability to articulate a shared vision of our goal that can provide a sense of ongoing purpose and connection. Attention to pedagogy itself, and to learning theory, could offer a new direction for English studies for the new century. Whether or not we can offer a rigorous definition of "literature," we could make teaching it our common cause, and teaching it well our professional work.

Objectives: What Do We Want Our Students to Learn?

Ask the average teacher of literature what she wants students to learn, and the answer will be "Romanticism" or "modern drama" or "literary theory." By and large, we are not accustomed to defining our objectives as actions or competencies – what students will be able to do, as well as understand – or as transferable skills. As one teacher comments, "Literature instructors often define their courses by the texts on their syllabi . . . not acts that students will be expected to perform."[11]

But the trends in pedagogy more generally are towards an emphasis on defining clear learning objectives for a course. Wilbert McKeachie reminds us that "the objective of a course is not to cover a certain set of topics, but rather *to facilitate student learning and thinking*."[12] That means coming at the subject from the point of view of the student, rather than the teacher. If, for example, our objective is "to introduce students to the development of literary theory," that is actually a "statement of what *we* want to do."[13] Overall, our objective in teaching literature is to train our students to think, read, analyze, and write like literary scholars, to approach literary problems as trained specialists in the field do, to learn a literary methodology, in short to "do" literature as scientists "do" science.

Moreover, the taxonomy of educational objectives developed by B. S. Bloom in 1956 posits a hierarchy of cognitive skills: knowledge, comprehension, application, analysis, synthesis, and evaluation. In every course, he maintains, teachers should strive for the higher-order objectives.[14] With relation to a literature course, thinking in these terms can lead to some startling transformations of teaching practice. For example, Linda Nilsen suggests, if we give students a definition of iambic pentameter, defining it becomes a low-order task of recall or comprehension. But if we give them examples of poems and plays and ask them to derive a definition of iambic pentameter, we are asking for a higher-order task of analysis and synthesis.[15]

Ultimately, learning objectives will guide us in forming assignments and carrying out assessments. Indeed, according to Paul Ramsden, merely listing objectives on the syllabus is not enough; "The most compelling reason for using aims and objectives . . . is that it forces us as teachers to make our intentions for student learning explicit. There ought to be a definite educational justification for every activity, every piece of content, that is present in a course of study. Tradition and habit are not satisfactory educational reasons."[16]

In Britain, university teachers must now provide learning objectives in order to have a course approved. But often, British teachers say, these "objectives" are not specific skills or techniques for students to master and apply, so much as general appeals to "understanding" or "knowing" about a particular group of texts. For American teachers of literature, active learning objectives seem quite difficult to imagine, and even questions about general goals are hard to answer. Roger Kuin points out that "we should never forget that in today's undergraduate teaching we are dealing with the vulnerable, the open, the intellectually virginal, the easily bewildered, the preoccupied, who have little background, little time, and little money. We should ask ourselves continually, what our goal is in teaching them the Renaissance. What do we want to accomplish?"[17]

A good question for other specialists as well. At Indiana University, Patrick Brantlinger reports, most of his English department colleagues when surveyed say that "the main goal of their teaching is to get their students to be 'critical thinkers.'" Brantlinger himself is critical of this goal as trendy non-

25

sense, common to other disciplines as well.[18] But we could say that we want students to learn a set of critical reading skills they can apply to the world of language, literature, and culture around them throughout their lifetime.

Robert Scholes (Brown) has proposed a reorientation of literary pedagogy towards rhetoric and reading. He believes that the craft of reading should become the central subject of departments of English, rather than any particular Great Books or political canons. This kind of pedagogy helps students "recognize the power texts have over them and assist the same students in obtaining a measure of control over textual processes, a share of textual power for themselves."[19] The enemy of "crafty reading," according to Scholes, is a "fundamentalist literalism" that threatens us everywhere, and that threatens human progress and freedom in our century.[20] One great advantage of this approach is that it shifts our thinking away from battles over content and towards process and skills, as well as the deeper reasons why we teach literature.

Assuming that we decide to adopt a program like the craft of reading, how do we break it down into specific, measurable, agreed, realistic, and timebound learning objectives? (Note that these form the acronym SMART, which some teachers use as a mnemonic.)[21] And how do we devise activities for students that will actively engage them in meeting these objectives? I'll be looking at some answers from experienced teachers to these questions in the following chapters on teaching literary genres. But on the whole, when we teach reading literature as a craft, rather than as a body of isolated information, we want students to learn the following competencies and skills:

1 How to recognize subtle and complex differences in language use.
2 How to read figurative language and distinguish between literal and metaphorical meaning.
3 How to seek out further knowledge about the literary work, its author, its content, or its interpretation.
4 How to detect the cultural assumptions underlying writings from a different time or society, and in the process to become aware of one's own cultural assumptions.
5 How to relate apparently disparate works to one another, and to synthesize ideas that connect them into a tradition or a literary period.
6 How to use literary models as cultural references, either to communicate with others or to clarify one's own ideas.
7 How to think creatively about problems by using literature as a broadening of one's own experience and practical knowledge.

8 How to read closely, with attention to detailed use of diction, syntax, metaphor, and style, not only in high literary works, but in decoding the stream of language everyone in modern society is exposed to.

9 How to create literary texts of one's own, whether imaginative or critical.

10 How to think creatively within and beyond literary studies, making some connections between the literary work and one's own life.

11 How to work and learn with others, taking literature as a focus for discussion and analysis.

12 How to defend a critical judgment against the informed opinions of others.[22]

Theories: How Should We Teach Literature?

If these are the skills we want students to acquire, how best do we teach them? Just as many teachers of literature have trouble defining literature, aren't sure why we teach it, and struggle to articulate exactly what we want students to learn, we are baffled when asked to describe our pedagogical theory. Very few teachers consciously and consistently apply any single theory, and the rest of us have no need to be monologic in our approach. But that doesn't mean that we can't profit by considering the range of identifiable formal theories that apply to the practice of teaching literature. I have divided them into subject-centered theories, teacher-centered theories, and student-centered theories. Subject-centered theories emphasize content and information, often presented as the "correct" answer. Teacher-centered theories focus on what the teacher must do or be, in order to facilitate education and emulation. Student-centered theories focus on the way people learn, and the organization of classroom process to maximize active learning. In practice, all of us combine variations of these theories, and apply them intuitively in relation to the circumstances of the course.

1 Subject-centered theories

The landmark description of subject-centered teaching is what the Brazilian educator Paulo Freire, discussing illiterate populations in third-world countries, called "the banking model" of education. In this theory, "education becomes an act of depositing, in which the students are the depositories and the teacher is the depositor . . . Knowledge is a gift bestowed by those who consider themselves knowledgeable upon those whom they consider to know nothing."[23] Sometimes called the "transmission" theory of teaching, this approach is primarily about transferring knowledge from the teacher to the student. Its main focus is content – what is taught. To some degree, all courses are subject- and content-centered, and teachers are expected to be knowledgeable about their fields. But some courses are more subject-centered than others, and carry also the implication of being determined and imposed by the teacher, whether from political or intellectual conviction.

Teaching from political conviction: "critical pedagogy"
In the late 1980s, some teachers were explicit and forthright about their belief that all teaching is political, and that their mission was to "shape the future of the nation by exposing students to the salvational power of the canon or the anticanon. In the grandiose designs of some progressive theorists, students who read carefully chosen emancipatory texts would leave their introductory writing courses with a lifelong awareness of systems of oppression based on race, class, and gender."[24] Ironically, this so-called liberatory, "critical" or "oppositional" pedagogy was often openly coercive and undemocratic. One composition teacher wrote in 1991, for example, that "because nearly every student who enters an American college or university is required to take a composition course, this project indeed has potential for bringing about social reform. However, because composition students are in some sense our captives, we must give up our traditional subscriptions to liberal tolerance if we are to bring about social change through them. We must also admit that we enact our own hegemonic desire when we use the required composition course to teach our preferred politics."[25] Cutting through the jargon, this means that indoctrinating students with leftist political ideas is a justifiable policy of teaching.

These theories carried over to literature as well as composition. In the late 1980s, for example, Cary Nelson, who was both writing a book on modern American poetry and cultural repression, and feeling "frustration with the Reagan-Bush era," devised and taught a course on modern poetry and the canon at the University of Illinois, Urbana. He gives a full and frank account of his intentions – perhaps fuller and franker than he would do in today's changed political environment – in a 1994 MLA anthology on using theory in the classroom. Nelson makes clear that although he allowed students to "air their views" and did not penalize them for making "objectionable remarks" on papers, he also "had an agenda for them, an agenda determined by my sense of where the country and the profession were culturally and politically, an agenda shaped by the cultural work I thought it was most useful for me to do." That cultural work was explicitly leftist teaching, "resistance teaching in a conservative department under a reactionary gov-

28

ernment." Whether the students had an agenda of their own is irrelevant to Nelson's decisions. Indeed, "some . . . responded enthusiastically; others resisted. A few have since told me or my colleagues that it was one of the two or three best courses they took here, but the evaluation form that complained 'If this was to be a left-wing indoctrination course, we should have been warned' no doubt captured the views of other students."

Nelson also "had a theoretical agenda that directed what I said about the readings we did," coming from Foucault and others, and a particular interest in the politics of canon-formation. He made the choices of what students would or would not read, and what they would write: "The students would go through the experience whether they wanted to or not. Thus they would be required to write essays about race or gender, essays about poems on working-class experience, whether or not they shared these concerns."[26] Although he was not inflexible, and dropped some texts that students really hated, Nelson viewed the content of his course as essential to its agenda.

Teaching from intellectual conviction

Nelson's very ideological and also teacher-centered course is an extreme example; but probably all teachers have strong interests, positions, and intellectual convictions about our subject. Although very few would admit to indoctrinating our students, most of us do come into class with an agenda and an approach to the work at hand. It is very difficult for specialists who have spent many years studying a writer or genre not to offer a golden key to interpretation. At Princeton, many bright undergraduate English majors indeed comment that they prefer to have a teacher give a strong reading of a work in class. Such presentations are a way for lecturers to model brilliance and originality, and, let's be honest, to compete with other faculty. While students may be encouraged to challenge the teacher's views, nonetheless the teacher's ideas and beliefs are at the center of this theory. Sometimes, too, discussion in these classrooms is Socratic, with the teacher leading students to discover predetermined clues and meanings.

As a young professor at Yale in the 1950s, Alvin Kernan recalls with irony how he lectured on *The Oresteia*: "I analyzed the trilogy in a formalist manner, mainly following a scenic and imagery pattern in which again and again light and hope flare up, only to expire into darkness and despair, and then to be relit once more . . . I did not hesitate to point out to the students that the struggle for justice that is Aeschylus's subject is still played out every day in our courts . . . this I told them, or tried to extract from them in later seminar discussion."[27]

An interesting account of the effects of such teaching comes from David Denby, the movie critic for the *New Yorker*, who returned to his alma mater,

Columbia University, as an adult to take its celebrated Great Books course. He was very impressed with the ardor and erudition of his first professor, Edward Tayler. Teaching *The Iliad*, Tayler "was working with the class on the structure of the huge poem, getting them to see large overall movements, and then smaller movements and patterns within limited blocks . . . Tayler didn't just tell the students what he wanted, of course. Imploring and urging, he pulled it out of them, asking leading questions, dropping hints, asking them to read passages aloud that have no apparent connection, passages spaced far apart in the book. At times, the class stalled, and he retreated from his point, literally stepping backward and letting his head drop for a moment before approaching from another angle, like a guerilla force making tentative forays through the jungle."

But Denby begins to sweat in fear that Tayler will call on him. "He was the kind of teacher who kept a student on the spot, trying to rattle the kid's brain around until the answer, locked in the bottom drawer of sloth and forgetfulness, suddenly fell out – something I always hated because at that point my brain would lock up."[28] Denby transfers to the section of a "looser" professor; Tayler's Socratic-warrior approach was brilliant but coercive. The former radical feminist, Ti-Grace Atkinson, now a lecturer at Columbia, was even more didactic; "she stood in front of the class with Aristotle's *Politics* in her hand, reciting long passages and expounding the text point by point. She explicated; the students listened."[29]

Oliver Arnold (Princeton) had his worst experience as an undergraduate with a teacher "who had clearly been immersed in left brain/right brain stuff, and this dominated the course. An extreme example of a hobby-horse course in which students experienced growing frustration." As a teacher himself, he doesn't "want to overpower students with my interpretations." But Arnold also feels that passionate conviction works well as long as there are also deliberate invitations to disagree. "Students really respond when they feel they are getting the full depth of what you feel and think, without having to assimilate their own thoughts to your point of view. So I'd teach with everything I've got, rather than offering ten equally good ways to read *King Lear*. I offer a strong point of view, but students are free to dissent."[30] Jeff Nunokawa (Princeton) also tries to balance "sharing convictions with openness to conflicting interpretations," to be "emphatic but receptive." His "agenda is always affected by what I'm thinking at the time," but "I never forbid a topic." He gives assignments, "getting them to participate in strange or new different ways."[31] Similarly, Martin Bickman writes about teaching *Moby-Dick*, "If we as teachers have our own line on the book, that line is useful only as a hypothesis to test in the interplay of a class and in scrutiny against specific passages, not as something to be inscribed directly in student notebooks without passing through their own critical sensibilities."[32]

Teaching the conflicts

In contrast to the individualistic approach of Socratic or critical pedagogy, Gerald Graff, who is now professor of English and Education at the University of Illinois, Chicago, has long been an advocate of a theory he calls "teaching the conflicts." In Graff's view, teachers of literature should deliberately include disciplinary and political conflicts in their classes, whether through team-teaching and actual debates, or through assigning critical readings that foreground internal debate. But the classroom should be an open, democratic, inclusive arena of political and critical conflict.[33] David Richter (Queens College, CUNY) agrees that "the best way to teach students to think for themselves – and to get them engaged in our conversation – is to be forthright about the irreconcilable differences within the profession over the interpretation and evaluation of texts, and to highlight in our teaching precisely these differences."[34]

In the foreword to Richter's textbook, *Falling Into Theory: Conflicting Views on Reading Literature*, Graff states the question most faculty have in mind: "Just what does 'teaching the conflicts' actually mean when it comes down to what an instructor actually does on an actual Monday morning in a roomful of actual undergraduates?" In *Beyond the Culture Wars* (1992), he explains his theory at greater length, showing how he teaches a class on "Dover Beach" organized around contesting critical interpretations.

But there have been a number of objections to Graff's theory as well. Does it narcissistically put English professors and our professional squabbles at the center of teaching, as Louis Menand suggests: "This represents a kind of perverse consummation of professionalism, the last refinement on the isolation and self-referentiality of academic studies; it makes what professors do the subject of what professors do."[35] Is it really a useful guideline to classroom practice? George Levine remarks that "there is very little critical or empirically based writing that works out in some detail what teaching the conflicts – however theoretically attractive on the surface – might entail."[36] Another criticism, from the left, is articulated by William Pritchard, who objects that Graff domesticates conflict by reducing it to critical spats: "by turning 'conflict' into a subject for the classroom, real conflict is defanged and too easily 'understood'."[37]

Finally, in Frederick Crews's parody of current theory, *Postmodern Pooh*, pragmatic Professor N. Mack Hobbes (a stand-in for Stanley Fish), explains that "Teaching the Conflicts was now all the rage in collegiate literary ped-

31

agogy. Previously, majors in English had been lurching haphazardly from one opinionated professor to another, picking up contradictory signals about the 'correct' way to interpret, say, *Paradise Regained* or 'Elegy Written in a Country Churchyard.' But under Teaching the Conflicts, all of these clashes of viewpoint are anticipated and given a curricular function." In a Teaching-the-Conflicts English department, "expectant nineteen-year-olds are told: 'Here is Husserlian phenomenology, here are the Jungian archetypes, here is Zizekian Lacanianism, here is Counterhegemonic Post-Gramscian Marxism, and here is the Deleuzoguattarian Anti-Oedipus; now *you* decide which hermeneutic should prevail.' "[38] On one memorable occasion, I turned my contemporary fiction course over to the nine preceptors. They each gave a five-minute presentation on the novel of the week, from nine different theoretical and ideological points of view. These conflicts came across to the students as more adversarial, political, and indeed hostile than intellectual, and that attitude of scorn for the writer, rather than any hermeneutic, is what they took away from the course. Without a clear purpose, teaching the conflicts may leave students feeling battered.

2 Teacher-centered theories

Teaching as performance

While many teachers, as I have said, feel nervous and guilty about the performative aspects of the job, performance is inescapable in teaching. Edward L. Rocklin, one of the advocates of the performance approach to teaching Shakespeare, reaches the same conclusions. "All teaching," he writes, "can also be seen as a form of performance." Thus "the crucial decision for every teacher . . . is not whether to think of teaching as a type of performance . . . but rather to decide (or consciously fail to decide) which type of performance to choose."[39]

Performance teaching is obviously a teacher-centered model, which stresses the instructor's speaking and acting abilities, along with his intellectual ones. Some teachers have the confidence and charisma to use the classroom as the venue for a one-man or one-woman show. Camille Paglia calls teaching "a performance art" in which the teacher is the model of humanistic inquiry, and describes her own style as including "frenetic Joan Rivers comedy routines." She believes that "teaching is when you have one person, a teacher in a room, doing improv with a class." In her memoir of her Binghamton professor Milton Kessler, Paglia describes him as a master teacher: "Kessler made me the teacher I am. He believed in the dramatic moment. Everything that you were, everything that you had ever seen or experienced pressed in upon the text in front of you . . . With the improvisation of great Jewish comedians like Lenny Bruce, Kessler would weave in and out of the class his own passing thoughts, reminiscences, disasters."[40] Paglia and Kessler are not the only teachers to mention stand-up comedy as a model. "The basic equipment for a classroom teacher is the same as for a stand-up comedian," writes Lionel Basney (Calvin College); "a striking voice, a direct gaze, and the inner freedom to say more or less anything that comes to mind."[41]

Jyl Lynn Felman at Brandeis has written the most exhilarating and thoughtful book about performative teaching. She insists that "there is a difference between performance for the sake of entertainment and performance that is integral to the process of learning." Felman believes that performative teaching allows the classroom to become a truly dynamic and dramatic space, a living theatre in which there will be intellectual eruptions. "At some point midsemester," she warns, "there will be a spontaneous combustion right in the middle of the show. The Professor as Leading Lady assisted by her TAs must be prepared to assist her audience the moment the academic volcanic eruption spews the hot molten lava of active, scintillating education around the room, covering everything in sight."[42]

The dangers of this volcanic theory of education come from its emphasis on what the teacher does. Lecturers as gifted as Paglia, Kessler, and Felman may be dazzling but they run the risk of monopolizing the spotlight. Moreover, teaching that is like stand-up comedy or postmodern performance art is seductive and exhilarating, but it can be very tricky to carry off. Not everyone can be a Paglia or a Kessler, nor do they need to be. Standing at a podium lecturing can be a fine performance; indeed, all good teachers are good performers, but not all good performers and comedians are good teachers.

I believe in the importance of performance, but I also think we need to give careful thought to the place of performance in an overall teaching practice. Officially, however, academia pays no attention to training literature professors to speak well. Partly because we do not interview or ask for information or videotapes, partly because recommenders will never mention speaking skills, I have seen graduate students embark on doctoral programs with speech impediments, crippling shyness, and incomprehensible accents. Rarely do graduate programs recommend speech therapy or training. In my experience, when graduate advisers have offered help, students have rejected it angrily.

Of course there are exceptions to all rules, and everyone knows at least one beloved but unintelligible professor. Eble tells a story of Ford Madox Ford lecturing inaudibly with great success at Olivet College, but warns that becoming a great professor by publishing 80 books is not the simplest route.[43] John Bayley became Warton Professor of English at Oxford despite a terrible stammer, but on the whole a stammer is not the best equipment for an academic lecturer, and if you are not a Ford or a Bayley, you are better off trying to speak clearly. Speaking skills can be learned. As Linda Nilsen writes, "those who start out weak in these skills but who work diligently on them can achieve impressive results within a year." Moreover, "like it or not, these public speaking techniques have a powerful impact on students' motivation and learning."[44]

Teaching as a spiritual journey

Parker J. Palmer, a professional specialist in education, is an advocate of a spiritual theory of teaching that is almost the direct opposite of performance. Palmer believes that "good teaching cannot be reduced to technique; good teaching comes from the identity and integrity of the teacher."[45] His model is teacher-centered too, but it emphasizes the teacher's inner being, his or her character and self-knowledge. In *To Know as We Are Known: Education as a Spiritual Journey*, he offers a vision of wholeness and community as an antidote to what he calls; "the pain of disconnection." The "spirituality of education," he declares, "will address the fear that so often permeates and destroys teaching and learning. It will understand that fear, not ignorance, is the enemy of learning, and that fear is what gives ignorance its power. It will try to root out our fear of having our ignorance exposed and our orthodoxies challenged – whether those orthodoxies are religious or secular."

While he begins with the teacher's spirituality, Palmer advocates a communal pedagogy and a community of learning that includes the teacher and the students. "The practice of intellectual rigor in the classroom requires an ethos of trust and acceptance. Intellectual rigor depends on things like honest dissent and the willingness to change our minds, things that will not happen if the 'soft' values of community are lacking." Instead, he recommends the creation of a "learning space" characterized by "openness, boundaries, and an air of hospitality." Most important is the hospitality which does not "make learning painless" but rather makes possible the painful things "without which no learning can occur – things like exposing ignorance, testing tentative hypotheses, challenging false or partial information, and mutual criticism of thought." These goals are enabled by the physical arrangement of the classroom, in a circle rather than rows; by depth rather than breadth of assignments; by the toleration and even encouragement of silence; teaching by questioning; and making space for feelings: "The teacher must make the first move in opening the space for feelings simply because the teacher has the power to do so. In whatever way seems natural, the teacher needs to convey something like this to the students: 'This is the place where it is safe for your feelings to emerge. I have feelings too, and I will make myself vulnerable by telling you some of them.' Teaching and learning are human enterprises and we must use human emotions in the learning process rather than letting them use us."[46]

Palmer begins his own courses with "extended self-introductions," and by speaking about his own emotions of "excitement and anxiety," his memories of being a student, and his invitation to students to speak to him in or out of class. He recommends that teachers develop the "discipline of standing outside their fields" by teaching in general education courses, and by becoming students from time to time themselves. When Palmer himself has become "someone else's student," he has been "reminded that education is not just a cognitive process . . . it is a process that involves the whole person, and so involves deep feelings as well. The feelings I remember most were frustration followed by boredom."[47]

Another version of this spiritual approach is Stephen Brookfield's "critically reflective" teaching, in which teachers keep logs of their reactions to their lives as teachers – moments when they "feel most connected, engaged, or affirmed," or, conversely, "disconnected, disengaged or bored;" situations that cause them "anxiety or distress," or events that take them by surprise.[48]

Again, not all of us will want to be so self-conscious about our reactions, but Brookfield's theory is a good counterbalance to the studiously objective and unemotional stance so familiar to a traditional style of teaching. David Perkins (Harvard), for example, recalls that for his generation, "to present literature impersonally and objectively was a cardinal point of classroom morality."[49] The morality of impersonal presentation also discourages the teacher's introspection and self-analysis.

3 Student-centered theories

Despite the attractiveness of subject- and teacher-centered theories, the impact of research on learning styles has led to a shift towards student-centered theories. Victoria Thorpe Miller (Alverno) observes that "in the literature classroom the emphasis is shifting gradually but inexorably away from the traditional exposure to 'great works,' with the teacher presenting background information and modeling a literary analysis that students will learn to emulate, toward an active, collaborative learning that takes place as the student confronts the text directly."[50]

Active learning is another name for the theory of teaching that emphasizes the student rather than the teacher. This approach to teaching has long been recommended by many educationalists around the world. Alfred North Whitehead talks of "the mastery of knowledge" that comes from having students be active doers and participants. John Dewey drily observes that teaching is a two-way transaction: "Teaching can be compared to selling commodities. No one can sell unless someone buys . . . [yet] there are teachers who think they have done a good day's teaching irrespective of what pupils have learned."[51] Paulo Freire advocates a dialogic, problem-solving pedagogy in which teacher and students "become jointly responsible for a process in which all grow."[52]

Here is Wilbert McKeachie's philosophy in brief: "What is important is learning, not teaching. Teaching effectiveness depends not on what the teacher does, but rather on what the student does. Teaching involves listening as much as talking. It is important that both teachers and students are actively thinking, but most important is what goes on in the students' minds."[53] In short, if students are not learning, no matter how brilliantly we perform or indoctrinate, we are not teaching. In order to be effective teachers we have to think about how students learn and how to help them learn.

Some student-centered teaching gives students a say in determining the syllabus. Anne L. Bower (Ohio State) had her introductory American literature class choose from an anthology which texts they would read.[54] William Gleason at Princeton has students in his course on American best-sellers vote on the final book on the syllabus. Such collective decision-making isn't essential. But in general, student-centered teaching makes the teacher a facilitator rather than a star. The teacher still performs, but the class is not primarily about the teacher's brilliance, omniscience, personality or originality on the podium. Indeed, for the student-centered teacher, the "lecture" and the "discussion" are transformed into "large-group teaching" and "small-group teaching."

Teaching from the microcosm

Among the many correlatives of active learning is the shift away from content to process and practice. Anxieties about content and coverage can lead some of us to pile on more and more reading, and struggle with a mass of undifferentiated material, rather than concentrating on what students get from such assignments. Parker J. Palmer's idea of teaching from the microcosm confronts the anxiety of coverage with some metaphors of his own. "Covering the field," he argues, "unconsciously portrays teaching as the act of drawing a tarp over a field of grass until no one can see what is under it and the grass dies and nothing new can grow." Instead of obsessing about the impossible act of assigning all the books, and telling the students everything we know, he advises, we should set clear priorities and boundaries for the all-too-short time we share with students. Rather than trying to cover a huge

36

terrain, including "everything practitioners know about the subject – information they will neither retain nor know how to use – I need to bring them into the circle of practice in that field, into its version of the community of truth. To do so, I can present small but critical samples of the data of the field to help students understand how a practitioner in this field generates data, checks and corrects data, thinks about data, uses and applies data, and shares data with others."

This theory is easily applied to the teaching of literature. "In every great novel, there is a passage that when deeply understood, reveals how the author develops character, establishes tension, creates dramatic movement. With that understanding, the student can read the rest of the novel more insightfully." Palmer concludes that this form of teaching-triage sets the best kind of intellectual example. "Teaching from the microcosm, we do not abandon the ethic that drives us to cover the field – we honor it more deeply. Teaching from the microcosm, we exercise responsibility toward both the subject and our students by refusing merely to send data bites down the intellectual food chain but by helping our students understand where the information comes from and what it means. We honor both the discipline and our students by teaching them how to think like historians or biologists or literary critics rather than merely how to lip-sync the conclusions others have reached."[55]

There is a useful guidebook for group discussion based on Palmer's ideas, which suggests some exercises for teachers considering teaching from the microcosm: brainstorming ways to teach a core concept of the field through shared teacher–student activity instead of lecturing, examining the pressures towards "coverage" and the ways it might be resisted and changed.[56] In general, teaching from the microcosm means tough thinking in advance about the aspects of the material that are most important for student learning.

4 Eclectic theories

But probably the most widespread theory of teaching literature is having no theory at all, and trying to make use of whatever will do the job. Steven Gould Axelrod writes that "as teachers, we need to be pragmatic, using whatever seems to work and not getting in the way of the book and the students."[57] Carl Woodring (Columbia) has described this approach as eclectic: "Until a better theory is built than we have now, the eclectic is the road to take." Woodring offers these suggestions for preparing to teach a literary work: "Begin by reading the piece (or tome) to discover changes in your own spontaneous response since you last read it. Ask, and then attempt to find out, what the author thought the purposes, the kind, and the distinguishing characteristics of the work to be. Then ask of the work itself how far it agrees with what you understand to be the author's expressed or customary intentions. Regard what it says to you as uncertain. Ponder possible meanings or significance, with dictionary as needed, of individual words and phrases, including the flunky words, *of, by, for, upon*. Distinguish the probable from the possible. Examine the structure, tropes, and rhetorical ploys. Bring all the contexts with which you can become familiar from genre through visual arts and psychology and sociopolitical history, all that might bear upon interpretation; while entertaining disagreement with received accounts of the work as a possibility, even as a professional opportunity, but not a necessity, ask how far these accounts survive your scrutiny. Ask what else in your being and life has influenced your comprehension and assessment."

Then the teacher should "carry this baggage into the classroom with you, but it is not a best step to begin the hour by unpacking it. Begin rather, even in a lecture room, by asking general questions ('How does reading this compare with other experiences you have had this year?')."[58]

The eclectic approach is probably the one most of us actually use in the classroom. But much of what Woodring says is about the teacher's preparation, rather than his practice. When he actually gets to describe the classroom, his theory is student-centered. He begins with an open-ended question that requires the students to make comparative judgments. When and how he uses his preparation is less clear, and perhaps that is the point – the eclectic teacher is ready to go with the flow, to use whatever is needed.

Personae: The Teaching Self

Finally, in addition to having a theory and a subject, all professors develop a persona, a public teaching self which may be either an exaggeration or an evasion of our private self. Some of these teaching personae become legends, at least for male professors who have always had privileged access to a wide range of authoritative or eccentric pedagogical roles. At the turn of the century, the Shakespearian scholar George Lyman Kittredge, at Harvard, cultivated the persona of "an Anglo-Saxon king speaking to his people," pacing the classroom with a long staff-like pointer, which he sometimes hurled like a javelin.[59] At Oxford in the 1920s, medievalist J. R. R. Tolkien, the author of *The Lord of the Rings*, "looked like a professor," in cords and a tweed jacket, smoking a pipe; but at home he sometimes mischievously appeared on his street dressed "as an axe-wielding Viking," and in class would begin "by walking silently into the hall, step up to the podium, and burst into the opening lines of Beowulf, the booming Anglo-Saxon stanzas filling the room: 'Hwaet we Gar Dena in geardagum.'"[60] Lionel Trilling at Columbia in the forties, according to Carolyn Heilbrun, was a "distant and disdainful" teacher who "spoke as a prophet – no less dramatic a word will suffice."[61] Often, more anxious souls, and insecure wizards of Oz, are hiding behind these prophetic masks. We know from biographies of Trilling that he was not so sure of himself. "Looking the part, while not being quite equal to it," confesses the distinguished academic Frank Kermode in his melancholy self-deprecating memoir *Not Entitled*, "seems to be something I do rather well."[62]

Female professors, of course, have personae too, although with the exception of a rare diva or prophetess, women's teaching personae tend to be more self-effacing or self-deprecating. Isobel Armstrong notes that the "transcendent effort of projection and drama in a classroom overrides my personal situation, simply erases it. I forget who I am." Gayle Pemberton writes ironically that at one point in her career, "I began to think of myself as 'Miss Chips,' some black, female, version of Robert Donat or Peter O'Toole from the movies, desexed, dowdy, reliable, kind."[63] Lisa Jardine admits that she "consciously cultivated a flamboyant lecturing persona, in my clothes and hair color (red, orange, pink) to make myself visible and to emphasize my difference from my reserved Cambridge colleagues. By the time I left Cambridge, in the late 1980s, I had enough sense of personal authority to abandon it, and to make more space for dialog with my students."

But whatever the persona, the most effective members of our profession are those whose literary theory is consistent with their teaching theory and practice – or at least not in conflict with it. Some professors, however, go through their whole careers without examining the gap between their teaching personae and their critical beliefs. In reading memoirs or descriptions of celebrated scholars or critics, in fact, I am often struck by the contradictions between the literary ideas and the teaching style. The most scandalous case in recent decades has been Paul de Man, "the embodiment of the great teacher," in Barbara Johnson's words, until he was posthumously discovered to have written for Nazi publications in his native Belgium during the war. De Man's students reverently declared that "he was never not teaching," but the lessons of Paul de Man turned out to have been quite different from what his disciples believed.[64]

The more usual example, however, is the teacher whose classroom practice is less impressive and coherent than his writing. Such a figure was Reuben Brower, a celebrated New Critic and famous teacher, who taught at Amherst and Harvard, and who influenced such major figures as de Man, Richard

Poirier, William Pritchard, and David Kalstone. Pritchard describes Brower's intellectual goal to be teaching students "what could be said, after careful looking and listening, about how words cohered to make a work of art." Brower believed that literary "designs were there to be discovered and appreciated for the way they promoted satisfyingly unified artistic experiences."

In the 1950s, Brower designed and led a famous course at Harvard called Humanities 6, or Hum. 6. According to Pritchard, then a TA in the course, "Brower delivered most of the lectures, including all the ones on interpreting poetry and poetic drama . . . Brower's lecture style took a bit of getting used to, since his voice was unimpressive, tending toward the monotonous and high-pitched. Often he had not finished delivering his lecture when the fifty-minute bell rang and he would ask for just a little more time. Students meanwhile were snapping the rings of their notebooks, preparing to head to another class or lunch. Brower would then hasten to cram, into the extra minutes, all the summary judgments and further speculations that he hadn't quite gotten into the first fifty. One was advised to listen closely to this extra inning, as it were, since it contained many of Brower's very best commentary. Yet many minds were doubtless elsewhere." Moreover, "often it was difficult to penetrate the manner and get Brower to listen to what you were saying, since he tended to decide quickly what you wanted, with the result that misunderstanding was likely . . . This habit of beginning to answer you before he had really listened to what you were saying made Brower vulnerable to some amused comments on the part of those who worked with him – but only behind his back. He was not a playful man or a good person to tease, even if you were bold enough to forget the difference in age . . . He was a man who jumped to conclusions."[65]

Although Pritchard does not say it, it seems to me that Brower's teaching was the antithesis of his literary theory. As a critic, he believed in coherence and closure, and preferred short tight forms like lyric poems. He was one of the great champions of close reading and insisted that students attend carefully and slowly to the verbal details of literary works. And yet, in his teaching, he resisted closure, simply could not manage it, threw away his conclusions; and was inattentive and hasty in his contacts with students. Brower's methods undoubtedly had an enormous influence on a whole generation of critics. But a professional culture that viewed teaching, or at least lecturing, as part of the total academic persona would have talked and thought about these discrepancies.

Another case of dissonance between the teaching persona and the critical thinker is Mortimer Adler, one of the founders and lifelong advocates of the Great Books program at the University of Chicago. Adler believed that teaching all students the great works of literature and philosophy was a democratic process that challenged elitist education and encouraged freedom of thought. But in his seminars, he "slapped the table and badgered students"; according to one outside observer, he carried out "as harsh a piece of brow-beating of a student" as he had ever seen.[66]

There are many ways we can be good teachers, but we need to be aware of the ways that our professed critical beliefs should inform our classroom personae. When the anti-establishment "Marxist" critic is authoritarian and rigid about the syllabus, or the feisty "feminist" critic shrieks in panic when faced with the slide projector, or the laid-back hippie who never wears a watch turns out to be a stickler about student deadlines, students will perceive the contradiction. In the final analysis, no theory of teaching can overcome a negative persona. And although a persona can protect you against the intimacy and threat of self-revelation in the classroom, it can also prevent you from achieving the real exchange of ideas that makes teaching memorable. If we want students to reveal themselves in our classes, then we too, as David Garvin says, must expose more of our "true selves in class, rather than [our] teaching personas."[67]

Chapter 3
Methods of Teaching Literature

Methods can be over-rated. As Marshall Gregory wisely notes, we can't "assume that one method or another will solve all problems . . . No one teaching method can meet all the demands of learning."[1] And then there's the ghost of T. S. Eliot whispering that the only method is to be very intelligent. Nevertheless, we can direct our intelligence more effectively if we are familiar with the basic methods and mechanics of teaching our subject.

A Teacher Prepares

The first step in teaching method is preparation, both of the course and the individual class. Such planning never takes place in an idyllic enclave cut off from the arbitrary external pressures of time, space, and money. Even designing a fresh new course involves us in consideration of enrollments, departmental turf battles, and resources. Walter Ong once cynically remarked that "course designing can become the academic equivalent of ambulance chasing";[2] but few of us can wholly escape from these crass considerations of trendiness and marketability. Douglas Howard, for instance, wanted to offer an elective special-topics course on "Victorian Literature and Evolution," but the curriculum committee did not think students would sign up for it. Eventually he came up with a course including canonical authors from Melville to Salinger called "American Psychos: Killers, Psychotics, and the Unstable in American Literature." Not what he had imagined in graduate school, when professors had told him about "preparing for the 'field' – it always sounded like I would be going off for war." Now he had to include popular fiction and films, and attract students to the course with theatrics. That was why, he explained, on the first day of class he was "being wheeled into my class standing on a hand truck wearing a Hannibal Lecter mask."[3] Let him who is without sin among us cast the first stone.

Our tendency in planning a syllabus is usually to block out the days available for teaching, and try to fit the books into this grid. The academic calendar of the semester invariably shapes intellectual and pedagogical decisions. Larry Danson observed that one of his Princeton courses had to be changed because he began on Thursday rather than Monday or Tuesday, and had to drop an introductory lecture. The academic calendar already impinges on teaching more than we realize. The shape of our mammoth literary anthologies has been designed to suit the teaching term; since 1999, the hefty two-volume (two-semester) format is being replaced by six-volume formats in the Longman and Norton literary survey anthologies, for the sake of flexibility; they can be "split 2-2-2 for quarter-system schools," as Longman editor David Damrosch explains, "as well as 3-3 for semester-system schools, and volumes can be used individually for period courses." In some anthologies, Damrosch also points out, "both the eighteenth and the twentieth century are generally foreshortened . . . simply because those periods are typically taught at the end of fall and spring terms, when teachers are pressed for time."[4] It would be ideal to teach both the *Canterbury Tales* and *The Waste Land* in April, but that's not very likely to happen.

Like an actor who has played the same part many times, a teacher prepares. But where is our Stanislavski? Who has studied the best way to prepare for a course or a class? The timing of the academic year, and the nature of memory, makes advance preparation problematic. A course has to be planned at least a semester in advance, so that books can be ordered, classrooms scheduled, students given a chance to enroll, and reserve reading set up in the library. But the gap between planning and teaching means that some of these decisions will have to be rethought or re-encountered when the term begins.

Beginning teachers often say that they will use the summer vacation to get a head start on their fall teaching, and even to write out all their lectures. But apart from the dubious wisdom of writing lectures out in full, preparing to teach so far ahead doesn't work. In a teaching journal kept by my husband, English Showalter, for example, he writes on September 17, 1996, "I have found from long experience that I cannot really prepare a whole course ahead of time and then just give it. If I reread all the literary works in August, the first ones would not be as fresh in my mind as I would like them to be when I go to class. I have of course read them all, in most cases several times, and taught them; some of them I have even written about extensively. In a pinch, I can get through a class with just my old notes, but I teach much better when I reread just a few days before the class, and make new notes. I always see things I missed before, and I'm much better able to respond to the students' questions and observations."

Kenneth Eble suggests that the best time to write, or rather re-write, a lecture, is right after you have given it. "The realities of a class are most apparent right when it's over, realities far different from a lecture on paper or even a tape-recorded lecture played back later. What worked, what didn't, what one wanted to do, what one will do next time – all these are vitally important to shaping effective lectures. And considering everything that can get in the way, preparing classes when the urge is strongest is virtually a necessity."[5]

Well, maybe. In any case, don't delude yourself that you won't need to come back to it just before you teach. Larry Danson has taught Shakespeare for many years, but when I asked him about preparation, he said, "Well, I read *Romeo and Juliet* yesterday and this morning. And also I spent a bit of time reviewing video tape, digitized, that you can look at on a computer. I move ahead and back rapidly. When I lecture, I prepare usually four type-written, double-space pages of lecture notes. I try to put them in groups – not more than four or five blocks. I time them out. I don't mean I rehearse. I just look at them and say: This is worth ten minutes; This is worth fifteen minutes. I try to have enough material so that I'm pushed to get it all in. I always overload a bit so that I have to hurry myself. I write notes in the margin – 11.10, 11.30. The other thing I have is passages I want to read out loud. Preparing the text – putting in the bookmarks – is very important for me."

Jyl Lynn Felman is a very different kind of teacher, who believes in improvisation and performance, but she too prepares detailed notes ahead of class. "The pedagogy of improvisation is not a breeze, something to substitute when you haven't had the time to prepare properly. On the contrary, good, effective improv only follows good, effective preparation. I am extremely conscientious when it comes to planning my classes by plotting out the entire three hours ahead of time. Every ten to fifteen minutes is diligently blocked out and highlighted in red on a yellow legal pad, listing facts, questions, comments, and a final synthesis. And I do not simply reuse these notes; each semester, the course material is updated and feedback from last year's class is incorporated into the new lesson plan."[6]

Preparing to teach is an intense form of research, and researching our subject is what professors have always excelled at and enjoyed. Can teachers prepare too much? "Teachers sometimes linger over preparation," writes Stuart Sherman (Washington University) "because they find there, in miniature, one of the main satisfactions of their vocation: the time to read, to think, and (with luck) to think new things and to prepare them for an imminent, experimental 'publication,' by word of mouth, more immediate than anything they can achieve in print. For many . . . to prepare a text for teaching is to go back to beginnings, to imagine a student's first encounter with a text, which of course in large measure means to remember one's own. The pleasure of anticipation gets curiously mingled with that of recollection."

Yet "over-preparation can sink a class as surely as no preparation at all; a teacher who sticks too closely to some remembered script may find little attention to spare for what's really going on in the room."[7] Part of the question is whether we teach from our area of research specialization, and make teaching a subset of research, or whether we make teaching an exploration for us as it is for our students. There are advantages and disadvantages to each approach. All of us have had the experience of reading a book the night before class, just one breathless step ahead of the students, and discovering that our teaching suddenly seems electric and the students are lit up with excitement. Teaching new material works, because we are teaching a way of reading, and modeling the way a trained professional thinks about understanding and analyzing literary texts.

Ann Thompson, who teaches at King's College London, is a Shakespearean scholar currently directing a graduate seminar on "Text and Playhouse" in conjunction with the Globe Theatre that exactly matches her research expertise and editorial work. But, she notes, sometimes when she is teaching *Hamlet* to undergraduates, "I find that I know it almost too well for the purpose; it is virtually impossible for me to imagine what it must be like to read the play for the first time, and I am capable of becoming impatient with students' perfectly reasonable desires to discuss topics which for me have become tedious through over familiarity." Thompson thinks that there is "much to be said for teaching outside one's own research area and even for sharing the students' experience of reading a text at high speed the night before the class!" Teaching new material, she points out, has led many professors to expand and redefine their research.[8]

Larry Danson agrees. "When I think of the best classes I've taught," he observes, "I always think of classes I taught a long time ago, when I was dealing with material that was fresh to me. And I shared a sense of excitement in being, quite literally, one step ahead of the students. I think it was when I was really grappling with the material as well as the ways to present."

45

His advice is to "try always to do something that you haven't done before." Similarly, Alex Zwerdling finds his favorite course is always the newest, the closest to his research; he believes that his teaching burns out after he has made up his mind on the critical problems. Wayne Booth says that "my own worst teaching has often been about those subjects on which I consider myself most expert. The novel that I have taught most ineptly, the one that I now refuse to teach, is one I did my dissertation on, *Tristram Shandy*. I just know too much about it – and I try to stuff it all in at once."[9]

The First Class

The semester too has a rhythm that affects our teaching, although it's an element literature professors too often overlook despite our concern with the temporal structures of stories. The first class, notes Laura Nash of Harvard Business School, "has its own dynamics of hospitality," including introductions and rituals of welcome.[10] Nevertheless, in the real world, the beginning of the semester can also be chaotic. There are more students than you expected, or fewer, or the wrong ones. The bookstore has just notified you that the first book on your syllabus is out of print. It is always too hot or too cold. Sometimes religious holidays interfere with the start of the term; at Princeton every fall, we had to schedule the beginnings of courses around the Jewish holidays.

Of course, as theoretically sophisticated, twenty-first-century professors of literature, we have learned to be skeptical of origins and beginnings, and to assume that every beginning refers us back to another point, that there is no such thing as the first reading, but only a rereading, and that we come to any text already programmed by other texts. Thus teachers may simply use the first class for administrative detail, going over the syllabus, explaining assignments, and so on. Sometimes they may even dismiss the class early, assuming that it is too soon to commence the real work of the term.

I think this is a big mistake. In the real world of the semester, the first class offers a never-to-be-recaptured moment of excitement and opportunity. This is your chance to preview the best material you have to offer. One of my models for beginnings is the lecture series on opera by the music critic William Greenberg, for sale on audio and video from the Great Teachers courses. Greenberg gives a brief explanation of the power of opera, and then plays "Nessun Dorma" from *Turandot* – an aria so thrilling that the most tin-eared listener must be swept away by it. Similarly, I think a literature course should begin, on the very first day, with a sample of the most stirring, memorable text you plan to read. Convey your enthusiasm to the students by sharing with them from the start the riches you have in store. Give them your best shot.

Specialists on pedagogy also suggest that the first class is a time to engage students in an activity, even in a large lecture. Take a survey; ask students what the terms of the course suggest to them. Steven Axelrod, who makes his students even in a large lecture course take an active role in answering and posing questions, uses the first class to describe his "modus operandi" and invite those who would prefer another to seek out an alternative class. Although few students leave as a result, such a declaration seems to make class members feel that they have made a conscious choice to undergo the experience and hence are responsible for what ensues."[11]

The instructor's behavior, body language, and appearance as well as his words in the first class transmit a set of expectations that has been called the "implicit contract" of teaching.[12] Everything, from what you wear, to whether you sit or stand, to your tone of voice conveys a message about the level of formality, difficulty, and flexibility of the course. Some teachers are hyper-aware of their staging. Jyl Lynn Felman notes that "color forever remains an important signifier in my role as a feminist professor – from what I wear to who sits in class . . . locating me at the center of an already decentered [racial] gaze." Among the colors she wears are purple, "burnt red, fire orange, sun-drenched yellow, sea-green turquoise and royal blue."[13] Jeff Nunokawa prefers not to be too self-conscious about staging choices. "There are rules, but you can't fully know them. I don't wear ripped t-shirts, but also not a suit. When I teach, the real me comes through." He has coped with the ambiguity of authenticity versus teaching persona by a paradox: "The way I've become a happy teacher is suspending consciousness during teaching itself but allowing it at every other moment."[14]

Testimony from students, and from our own experience as learners, shows that much as we would rather ignore these lowly semiotic clues, we are very much aware of them. For example, here is *New Yorker* critic David Denby, back in school as an adult, trying to psych out the implicit teaching contract of Anders Stephanson in the Columbia Great Books course: "The students couldn't make him out yet. He was handsome, slender, about forty years old, with blond hair and blue eyes and rather dazzling smile, and he wore faded jeans and, under a dark jacket, a white T-shirt. To my eyes, the T-shirt was a rakish touch, especially with the black jacket. A youthful biker-intellectual, then? No, I couldn't see him slopping beer on the table. When he talked, the rhythms and vocabulary were the purest advanced academese. The accent was almost British, the manner emphatic – boisterous yet stern in British academic style."[15] And this is all before Stephanson has given an assignment or a lecture, or led a discussion.

Oliver Arnold admits that he is "fully conscious" of his teaching persona, and tries to pay some attention to what he wears, at least to "vary a bit." On one hand, he hasn't "worn a tie more than twice this semester," but when he feels that he has been too informal, "I try to dress like an adult next time and reassert some dignity and authority."

Difficult as the implicit contract may be to control, it is very hard to negotiate once it has been established, so we need to think about it carefully. In a discussion course particularly, Abby Hansen writes, "many of the disasters that befall teachers . . . from late-semester apathy, to unnerving emotional outbursts, spring from underlying flaws in the implicit contract."[16] We may speak softly and carry a big grading stick; we may act tough but be unprepared to back up our demands. In teaching, what students see should be what they get.

Teaching also has an explicit contract, of course, and ideally this should be as full as possible, in order to anticipate the sorts of problems that will inevitably arise. What are the deadlines for papers? The penalties for lateness? The policies on reading paper drafts? The criteria for grades? The rules on missing or cutting class? Your availability after hours, on weekends, during vacations? Some of this can be negotiated at the beginning with students. For example, what do they think is the right response if a student arrives late, falls asleep, reads the campus newspaper? Will there be questions allowed during the lecture?

You will never anticipate everything. But every course is a fresh start, a chance to start anew, to get it right. Michael Berubé suggests that the beginning of each semester is an opportunity for self-renewal. "Buddhists speak of learning to see the world with 'beginner's mind' and that's precisely what you have to do every semester: Begin again, from scratch, knowing that anything can happen – seeing those 10, or 50, or even 500 students, like the 2,000 students you've seen before, with beginner's mind."[17]

The Rhetoric of Teaching

1 Lecturing

Most people think entertainment is having a nice laugh. But you can be entertained by a lecture.

> Ron Howard, *director of* A Beautiful Mind

For years, I have introduced my off-campus academic lectures with a line from Malcolm Bradbury's brilliant satiric novel, *Rates of Exchange* (1983):

48

"A good friend will come to see you in prison, but a *really* good friend will come to hear your lecture." Lecturing is ubiquitous in higher education, although there is a remarkable consensus among teaching specialists on its extensive drawbacks. The lecture has to confront problems of attention span, memory, and distraction, and these are not simply problems of poor or unmotivated students, but basic human issues of perception and retention. Despite our best intentions, only rarely can most of us focus on the full 50-minute presentation. Studies of attention-span and retention for lectures agree that attention levels are highest during the first ten minutes, and drop off rapidly thereafter. Material presented in the middle of a lecture is retained less well than that at the beginning or the end. Nevertheless, attention levels and memory can be stimulated if there are breaks, or changes of approach, about every 15 minutes; and if key points are signaled, as "advance organizers."[18]

According to Donald A. Bligh, in *What's the Use of Lectures?*, even "the inspirational function of lectures is asserted more often than it merits. Admittedly, most of us can remember a few lectures that stood out and influenced us as students, but they are usually few compared with the total number of lectures received." Bligh points out that "during discussion students are more attentive, active, and thoughtful than during lectures." Yet "some people place faith in their lectures to stimulate thought and expect thinking skills to be absorbed, like some mystical vapors, from an academic atmosphere."[19]

Teachers of literature know this first hand, because we have all endured the conference papers and public lectures that illustrate the worst aspects of lecturing – narrow readings of unfamiliar texts, pointless cultural expositions, narcissistic display. In nine cases out of ten, everything the lecturers supposedly know about reaching an audience vanishes under the pressures of intellectual competition or prevailing conference fashion. As someone who finds most academic lectures an ordeal, I was relieved to read Martin Bickman's confession that "I blush to say it, but I was never tired or bored by my own lectures. And yet I know I cannot keep my mind from wandering after about a half hour of someone else's lecture, no matter how good it is."

Bickman pondered this paradox, and came to the conclusion that lecturing is an active form of thinking *for the teacher*, but a passive form for the listener. "This realization helped explain why often what I thought were the most brilliantly original parts of my lectures lagged the most for the students. I was thinking things out for the first time, discovering what I had not seen before, but these ideas by their very nature were not yet in a form that was particularly clear or incisive to my listeners. These were also my

49

most enthusiastic moments of lecturing, but clearly they were not the ones that created the most enthusiasm in the students . . . Although I feel strongly that good, short, well-prepared lectures can be useful, it is also important to be aware that we are always embodying our values in the classroom by what we choose to do, and that to lecture is to value having thought over thinking, the transmission of knowledge over its making."[20]

Even the greatest lecture – great, that is, in terms of brilliance, originality, comprehensiveness, and eloquence – can be more intimidating than inspirational. Parker Palmer, who values spirituality above the polished performance, is "not against lecturing, listening, and memorization. Done properly in the right context each of them has a role in creating the community of relatedness called truth." The danger, though, he warns, is that often lecturing is "authoritarian," listening "unengaged," and memorization "mechanical."[21] In *W;t*, the Pulitzer Prize drama by Margaret Edson, a demanding professor of seventeenth-century literature, dying of ovarian cancer, re-examines the priorities of her life and career. One of her teachers – now an intern in the hospital – recalls that "She gave a hell of a lecture. No notes, not a word out of place. It was pretty impressive. A lot of students hated her though." In fact, he concludes, "it felt more like boot camp than English class." When I started teaching at Princeton in 1984, and had to adapt to a two-lecture-plus-weekly-discussion format, the lecturing style most admired by undergraduates – a polished performance that reached its intellectual climax at the bell – seemed very masculine to me. Women, I suggested to the students, could climax more than once.

Another shortcoming of lecturing is that it cannot address the individual concerns and needs of students, but has to be pitched to a generic student. Michael Berubé taught an undergraduate honors course on postmodernism and American literature at the University of Illinois. On his bad lecturing days, he recalls, "I was teaching to the six – the six (or five, or seven) students who came to class already caring about literature, criticism, narrative, and history. Of the other 30, 12 or so were intermittently engaged by the course and will probably remember it fondly for some time, and the remaining 18 were by turns surprised, stimulated, puzzled, and bored." Berubé concludes that "it is quite impossible to inspire in undergraduates the single-minded attention, the devotion to every professorial train of thought" that can be expected of graduate students.[22] Indeed, and I suspect that Berubé is over-estimating the attention span and devotion of graduate students as well. But can we justify teaching six students out of thirty as a necessary consequence of undergraduate inattention? It is the responsibility of the teacher to try to engage all of the students, even if that is an impossible goal.

50

Some outstanding teachers prefer lectures, and have thought hard about why. Bonnie Zimmerman, of the University of California at San Diego, declares: "I believe in telling students what they ought to think. I tell them, 'I'm going to preach to you, because I want you to think about the meaning of books and I believe that literature makes you a better person. That is why we read, that is why I go to school.'" She explains her process: "I've basically taught the same syllabus now, with tinkering, for seven or eight years. I have the syllabus where I want it. I teach the same course every semester – women in literature – and I think that it works very well, the students seem to think that it works very well, and I know the literature inside and out. I don't use notes, I don't even necessarily need to use the book. I'm talking to them and focusing directly on them, and I think that's important; if you are going to lecture you have to be totally focused on the students. I also convey a great enthusiasm for the material and it is infectious. I ask a few pointed and direct questions, and have an overall sense and plan for how I want the class to go. And students are very predictable. They ask the same questions all the time. They have practically the same responses all the time . . . I show them how to see something in the poem and by the end of the semester I expect that they will be able to do it by themselves or at least do it better than before."[23]

The fabulous Ms. Mentor (the persona of Emily Toth, Louisiana State University), who writes a regular advice column to academics on the website of the *Chronicle of Higher Education* and has written an advice book for women in academia, also likes to lecture. "Ms. Mentor happens to enjoy the theatrical side of teaching," she explains, "for it makes use of her native grandiosity . . . She can lecture with equal brilliance to one hundred and fifty or to one poor advice seeker." But for those less well-endowed by nature, Ms. Mentor offers some reassurance: "It is far easier to lecture than to try to wrest any kind of discussion from recalcitrant or puzzled or very large audiences. A lecturer can write on the board, or pace, gesture, dramatize, grimace, snicker. She can use her voice as an expressive tool: Ms. Mentor, who possesses a naturally warm and mellow contralto, has sometimes burst into song, providing transcendent moments for her auditors."[24]

Even if we lack Ms. Mentor's vocal gifts, if teachers want to make the most of lecturing, we need to understand how to make a lecture memorable. There is good, and consistent, advice to be found in pedagogy handbooks. They recommend the following:

- a clear structure and outline
- a statement of objectives

- frequent signposts
- handouts, especially with spaces for students to answer questions, solve problems, or add their own notes
- a shift of material or approach every fifteen minutes
- strategies for student participation – buzz groups, problem-solving, giving examples, Q & A
- use of audio-visual materials, with instructions about what to look for
- student votes on various positions.

Rob Pope, a principal lecturer in English at Oxford Brookes University, teaches on Friday afternoon – "the dead spot." But he is determined to make the time slot work for his course on English "in a contemporary global context." Pope specializes in "interactive teaching," and encourages his students "to rewrite classic texts in contemporary styles or different cultural contexts." He begins the session by asking the students to think of a caption for a drawing he has put on the overhead projector – an ice breaker and a "serious game" that gets things going.[25]

Even with an audience of several hundred, student-centered teaching looks for strategies to make learning active – through buzz sessions, problem-solving, debates, interviews of a guest, in-class writing, structured questioning, one-minute response papers, and other techniques. McKeachie's chapter in *Teaching Tips* on "Teaching large classes" offers many helpful suggestions, and stresses that "active learning does not necessarily involve only student talking, writing, or doing; what is important is active *thinking*."[26] Richard Felder suggests occasionally pausing in a lecture, and assigning students five minutes to work at a related question or task in groups of two or three at their seats.[27] Isobel Armstrong describes herself as "not a very self-reflexive teacher," but even in lectures, she uses "debates, quizzes, and other activities to make students participate."

I have to confess that lecturing in a large auditorium at Princeton I have never been able to implement buzz groups and student group work; the students resist it too much. But I have had much more success using frequent video clips, bringing in writers for the students to interview, using handouts, inviting preceptors to give ten-minute mini-lectures, and using personal anecdotes. As Kenneth Eble writes, "It is surely among the simplest truths of public speaking that the audience's interest picks up when the discourse turns personal. Thus, a deliberate introduction of the personal is a teaching technique as vital as the use of illustrations and examples, which themselves gain in interest as they are drawn from the teacher's personal experience."[28] Enthusiasm, energy, humor, all help maintain interest and assist memory.

2 *Leading discussions*

Students do not always perceive the differences between the lecture and the discussion. One student commented on his evaluation, "it seems to me that the main difference between lectures and seminars was that in seminars the tutor sat down."[29] All too often, a so-called discussion class is just another opportunity for the teacher to do all the talking.

Few of my own courses as a Bryn Mawr undergraduate in the 1960s involved discussion, even though classes were small. But a social psychology course I took at Haverford on "Small Group Dynamics" was probably more important for my career as a teacher than anything else I studied. The seminar itself became the laboratory as each week's reading predicted the power dynamics, rearrangements, tensions, and upheavals of our small group, and we saw in our own group dynamics how seminars form, norm, storm, and perform.

I realized then, watching our professor set up the discussions but stand back and let us follow our own path with occasional questions and suggestions, that preparing to lead a discussion is very different from preparing to give a lecture. "Preparation," David Garvin explains, "now means exploring multiple paths of inquiry, rather than mapping out a single linear flow . . . When the instructor must anticipate the probable flow of discussion and plan for in-class dynamics, preparation is a far more complex task than it was when content alone was king."[30]

In the class discussion of our dreams, one professor has fantasized, we would "ask the perfect question and not say another word."[31] The perfect opening question should be one that everyone can answer, but that leads into other important issues of the work. Questioning, listening, and response, are what C. Roland Christensen of Harvard Business School, the world authority on case-method teaching and a pioneer teacher of teachers in workshops and seminars, calls "the panels of a triptych" for discussion leaders. "Mastery of questioning," he observes, "does not begin and end with framing incisive queries about the day's material. It requires asking the right question of the right student." He offers a typology of the kinds of questions that are most productive in discussion classes: open-ended, diagnostic, information-seeking, challenging, action-seeking, predictions, hypotheticals, and generalizations.[32]

Harvard has produced a videotape of Christensen teaching, with comments from colleagues and students, which is a terrific way of starting a teaching workshop of your own. In the classroom, as the *Harvard University Gazette* wrote when he died in 1999, Chris Christensen "was a true artist, moving his arms gracefully like the conductor of a symphony orchestra, as he posed questions to students, listened carefully to their replies, and then responded – all within the rapid give-and-take context of an energetic and rigorous discussion."[33] When we watched the video in the Cotsen seminar, reactions to Christensen's mild, gentle, avuncular style of eliciting contributions from his group so charmed one graduate student that he tried to channel Christensen in his own precept, right down to the body language and hand movements: "Since we saw this video, I've been trying to use the directionality of my body language more fully. I noticed that what made C. R. C. so captivating was the way in which he swiveled towards whoever was talking, and then back again towards whoever he wanted to respond, holding his hands up in the air. I had the feeling that he was carrying something from student to student." He tried copying these gestures in his precept; "because I was 'carrying' comments from one student to another, suggesting a kind of communality of theme, everybody really seemed to get involved and engage each other in a deep way. I'm amazed that such a small change in my style resulted in such an active discussion."

Christensen strongly believed that effective teaching can be learned, and that even more than lecturing, it demands putting the students' needs ahead of one's own ego. Above all, it requires the establishment of a learning community, one of trust, constructive response, and intellectual partnership. He was among many specialists who recommend having students introduce themselves, and taking some time at the beginning of a course to let the class relax, get to know each other, and bond. A skeptical TA found that this method paid off: "I truly appreciate having taken that leap of faith and focusing on process over content in the first two weeks. I had been kicking myself for not doing a close-reading approach during the *Canterbury Tales*, but I see now how much more comfortable they are with one another; they can let me slip into the background. The readings they offer are not theoretically deep all the time, but they are always surprising each other and me."

Some teaching specialists recommend asking students to take a few minutes to write their answers to the opening question before sharing them. Jessica Richard found that this technique worked well: "I had them write for five minutes about three poems. This was the first time I did in-class writing. I was amazed at how this little bit of reflection helped them not only to make interesting comments, but also to talk to each other, not just me. Suddenly they had a reading of their own, and when someone said something similar or opposite, they jumped in and told us what they had written and how it related to what had just been said."

Another recommendation is to have students pair off and discuss the questions together before they speak. Again, TAs discovered that this method worked well: "At first I was nervous that I was using up too much class time on pairing and sharing, but it was as if we got two minutes back for every minute we spent. Each of the five groups had great things to say and time enough to say them and everyone was finally talking to each other instead of mostly me or the room."

Experienced teachers develop their own techniques for enabling open discussion. William Gleason (Princeton) takes notes in class of what students say. "One of the goals of taking notes is to help my memory, so that I can go back and link concepts with people; another is for students to learn as quickly as possible that I am not the center of attention, and focus on developing arguments along with their classmates."[34] Mark Hanson (Princeton) tries to set a tone of informality, and help students "get over their initial reaction of resistance to postmodernism or denial of its relevance." He encourages them to "draw connections between things that are familiar – to talk about tattooing and body art – and to move from that to postmodern theory." Lisa Jardine learned how to ask questions when she was an interviewer on BBC's *Nightwaves*. "We were taught how to question people, to open a space for them to give good answers. You have to know who you are talking to, and learn not to speak too much. It enhanced my teaching no end, and I've never looked back since."

3 Modeling

When I suggest that teachers of literature need to do some modeling, I don't mean that we show off our wardrobes, although attention to costume in the classroom is never a bad idea. I mean instead that students will learn better if we not only explain what skills and techniques we expect them to master, but also show them models and examples. As Bligh notes, "if you want to teach a behavioral skill, at some stage the student should practice it . . . You might think this principle is obvious. And so it is, to ordinary people. But it is quite beyond some of the most intelligent people our educational system has produced. They want their students to do well in examinations, but they never give practice in doing them."[35] In assigning papers, we can xerox or make available in the library examples of outstanding student papers from the past, or even papers we have written ourselves. Providing models of good writing, and allowing time for students to discuss them, can help establish realistic goals. Even before we are asking students to write, we can talk to them about how to use their texts, how to do useful annotation, how to underline, how to keep a running index in paperbacks of key terms, characters, and plot lines.

One fundamental critical technique we expect literature students to learn is *close reading*. Some teachers see close reading as primarily an ideological term connected to the New Criticism. For example, Andrew Bennett and Nicholas Royle, in the glossary of their *Introduction to Literature, Criticism, and Theory*, define it as a method which excludes attention to "the historical and ideological context, the biography or intentions of the author and so on . . . It assumes that the function of reading and criticism is simply to read carefully what is already 'there' in the text."[36] Terry Eagleton jokes that close reading "seemed to imply that every previous school of criticism had read only an average of three words per line," and that "it encouraged the illusion that any piece of language . . . can be adequately studied or even understood in isolation."[37] Other teachers are suspicious of close reading as a genuine technique. John Schild, for example, argues that "as a pedagogical goal of literary studies, close reading remains a hazy concept. The term functions largely as a catachresis, a placeholder, substituting for a more exact description of interpretive strategies."[38]

But I take a more positive view of what this term means, and of its usefulness in teaching. The close reading process, or *explication de texte*, that we use in analyzing literary texts does not have to come with the ponderous baggage of the New Criticism, or with political labels. Before or along with attention to factors outside the text, students have to understand something about the verbal, formal, and structural elements of the words themselves. Close reading can be a neutral first step in understanding literature. But this sort of reading is far from natural or intuitive, and if we want students to learn how to do it, we need to give them both models and practice.

In her handouts for a Princeton survey course on English literature, Jessica Richard (now at Wake Forest) gave questions for close reading of a sonnet: "Characterize the verbs in each sentence. List all the similes and metaphors. How would you describe these figures? How is the 'volte' used? Is there a marked pause or turn at the start of the ninth line, or does it come elsewhere? What is the effect of this? What is the relationship of the couplet's meaning to the quatrains? Develop a thesis statement about the poem's images."

4 New technology

Some of us have just proudly mastered the slide projector and the VCR, and here come PowerPoint and the electronic classroom. The new technology is no panacea or shortcut to success. "The more electronic stuff you use," warns Larry Danson, "the more time it takes. The deeper I've gotten into this stuff, the more I've wanted to pull the plug and say 'Destroy the machines!' I'm joking, but it takes an awful amount of time. Every electronic tool makes more work; it's not a labor-saving device in any way." Danson spent an entire summer planning and designing the website for his first-year Shakespeare course. If technology is going to work, it has to be carefully planned and thought through; not "pedagogical parsley added decoratively to the edge of the platter of learning, but . . . part of a fundamental reconstruction of what we consider learning to be, how we think learning is acquired, and what the appropriate means are for demonstrating that one has it."[39]

Campus computing and IT centers are the best sources for information and guidance on how to use the new technology in teaching, and there are now numerous books of theory and advice, in addition to websites.[40] I have now used a course website for several years, with hyperlinks to useful sites, definitions of key terms, assignments, advice for writing papers, and other information. I also encourage students to email me with questions and comments, and promise to answer any questions I receive before 10 p.m. each night. Email means that I am accessible to students even when I am not in my campus office.

But the most rewarding and revolutionary aspect of the new courseware has been its interactive capacities. The Blackboard software used at Princeton provides an easily programmed home page for each student on the roster, complete with photograph. I have students complete these the first week, and they are a terrific way for me to learn about the students and for them to learn about each other. I am also able to set up electronic discussion boards for each precept. Students are required to post a weekly pre-precept message, as long or short, complex or informal as they wish, in response to the reading. These discussion boards have become real conversations, and they also serve to get students writing from the very beginning. Often, preceptors (who kick off each week's discussion with a very general question) use the postings to help students define paper topics.

The Business of Teaching

1 Grading

Grading is one of the most fraught areas of university teaching for everyone involved – students, teachers, administrators, parents, and politicians. I've already commented on the furor over grade inflation currently receiving publicity from journalists and politicians. Grade inflation is an educational concept only applied to the young. As adults, paying for education or training, we would be indignant at the idea that most of us are expected to fail.

We assume that good teaching means good learning. But these expectations drop away in the context of the university, where a keen belief in tough assessment and grading goes along with what Paul Ramsden calls "a profound ignorance about measurement and testing and their relation to teaching and learning."[41]

Ramsden also emphasizes the fallacy of trying to make your subject and your grading tough. "Truly awful teaching . . . " he writes, "repeatedly displays the classic symptom of making a subject seem more demanding than it actually is. Some people may get pleasure form this kind of masquerade. They are teaching very badly indeed if they do. Good teaching is nothing to do with making things hard. It is nothing to do with frightening students. It is everything to do with benevolence and humility; it always tries to help students feel that a subject can be mastered; it encourages them to try things out for themselves and succeed at something quickly."[42] Low grades do not motivate students to work harder; they are much more likely to discourage and lower interest.

Nonetheless, grading is an inherent and inescapable aspect of university teaching, no matter how much we may dislike it. Richard Miller (Rutgers) offers a forthright and sensible defense of the necessity of grading: "*All* teaching positions in accredited programs require a terminal assessment of student work. This unavoidable process of soliciting, assessing, and responding to student work constitutes the core of the business of education, whether one is teaching entry-level students how to navigate academic prose, assisting advanced undergraduates to construct independent research projects, guiding doctoral students towards the successful completion of a dissertation, or commenting on submissions to an academic journal."[43] Obviously, grading is a much easier task if you have a clear idea of what the exam or the paper or report is supposed to demonstrate. The best and most comprehensive guidebook to grading I know is *Assessing Student Learning in Higher Education*, by George Brown, with Joanna Bull and Malcolm Pendlebury (Routledge, 1997).

In my pedagogy seminars, issues about grading papers came up most frequently. Giving students models of what you expect and how you will grade helps. Stephanie Smith has students grade a sample student paper, as part of a one-hour paper-writing workshop. We also did sessions on paper titles, using lists of titles from past student work; and on defining a topic. The more time teachers can spend preparing students for what is expected of them, the better. But there will always be problems. My advice is to separate the paper from the person, without apologizing for the grade or backing down; to stay positive and concrete. A preceptor responded to an angry student by email: "I understand that you are disappointed by a C+. Please remember that I can grade the paper only on its own terms; I know you to be intelligent and hard-working; nevertheless a paper needs to contain a clear thesis clearly argued and well-supported, and yours did not." He offered to help the student with drafts of the next paper, and indicated that improvement would be reflected in the final grade.

Although some teachers allow students to rewrite papers and resubmit them, for both practical and pedagogical reasons, I am against it. The temptation is for the teacher to feel adversarial or defensive, or to start bargaining over a different grade. I recommend instead that TAs encourage students to set clear goals for the second paper and have them apply in that what they have learned from criticism. Reading drafts of papers can become a real drain on teachers' time, and also set up expectations of higher grades that may be awkward; one solution is to limit reading of drafts to students who fall beneath the B level after the first paper.

Finally, prompt feedback is a key element in making grading useful for student learning. The most meticulously marked and carefully annotated paper, returned a month after it has been written, will make less impact on the student's improvement than briefer comments returned immediately. I try to schedule papers with rapid feedback in mind, and to work with preceptors to agree on the date for returning student work and the kinds of comments we can make within these constraints. A model that has worked well is to begin with a positive comment, and then to indicate three specific areas for improvement. Teachers keep a copy of these comments for themselves as guidelines for grading the next assignment.

Overall, as Kenneth Eble recommends, "teachers can and need to be inventive . . . in finding ways to evaluate performance that identify the particulars by which performance can be improved . . . The shift from grading to useful evaluating, from classifying and certifying students to teaching them, will begin when we recognize that grades are a peculiarly academic hang-up."[44]

2 Housekeeping

When I was directing the Cotsen Teaching Seminar at Princeton, one of my goals was to demystify all the backstage apparatus of teaching, and to show graduate students that lectures and discussion plans do not spring fullborn from the head of Zeus or Minerva. Every semester, I would have the students over for dinner and show them my home office and teaching files, an act that felt as intimate as opening my closet or bureau drawers. I have never seen anyone else's teaching files, except my husband's. His are immaculately labeled, all the same elegant beige, and filled with neat pages; mine are a garish rainbow of filing folders, stuffed with longhand notes, xeroxes, cartoons, clippings, and print-outs. But they work for me, and everyone needs to find a method that suits their own needs.

I organize my teaching notes by course (a file drawer to a course); by theme, author, and individual texts. In one drawer, for example, goes the *fin de siècle*, with folders on topics including aestheticism, decadence, the New Woman, imperialism, and individual authors from Aubrey Beardsley to Zola, with multiple folders for specific works by Stevenson, James, Hardy, Wilde, Wells, and others. In other drawers, I keep the course materials for contemporary fiction, the American short story, American women writers, and conspiracy theory. For each course, I keep a general folder. It holds past syllabi, paper topics, and exams; handouts, including maps, author biographies, definitions, and critical excerpts (although I now put most of these on my course website rather than copying and distributing them); and copies of outstanding papers from previous years that I can use as models.

I also have cases of slides, and videos for each course grouped on my office shelves. The slides, of writers, their homes, objects, book covers, book illustrations, paintings, and the like, I use less now that I have the classroom technology to show video clips; I've given my collection to my department, and someday they will be indexed and digitalized for everyone to use. Finding videos is a matter of luck and effort; I read catalogs from the video dealer Facets in Chicago, and also buy videos in England and France that I can have reformatted for American VCR. I try to assemble a wide variety of videos to use for clips in the classroom – film versions of books and stories; biographies; interviews; historical background; illustrative materials. I always try to have more than one video version of a text, so that students can compare. For example, I may do a class on Stevenson's *Treasure Island* which compares the Long John Silver of Robert Newton to that of Charlton Heston, or look at the imagery in four transformation scenes of *Dr Jekyll and Mr Hyde*.

In my department office, separate from the content matter of teaching, goes all the paraphernalia of assessment and bookkeeping. I have files of my own student teaching evaluations for many years back; my grade sheets; and alphabetical folders of letters of recommendation, although invariably when I hear from a former student who urgently wants ten copies of the original letter updated, I can't find it. Now these letters are all stored on the computer. Some teachers recommend keeping permanent notes on individual students and copies of all your comments on their papers; I don't have space enough and time to keep them myself – I throw them out at the end of the term – but I do ask students to supply some information and copies of papers when they need a recommendation.

The methods of teaching are more or less the same for every field and discipline. What makes teaching literature special is not that we use lectures or discussions or models, but that the subject matter itself suggests ways of applying these methods. In the following four chapters, I will be discussing the genres of literary study – poems, plays, fiction, and theory – and showing how they contain their own guidelines for classroom method and practice.

Chapter 4

Teaching Poetry

Teaching poetry offers the literature instructor some of the most fundamental, immediate, active, even physical ways to engage students in learning. Ironically, not very long ago everyone assumed that teaching poetry was at the center of teaching the mysteries of literature, a sacred rite of the New Criticism, conducted in an atmosphere of intense and manly collegial consensus. Frank Ellis remembers teaching Freshman English at Yale in the years after World War II. "The textbook was Brooks and Warren's *Understanding Poetry* (1938). There were a dozen sections, of which Cleanth Brooks himself was the boss. Many of the students were veterans. The instructors met with Cleanth once a week to hammer out the school solution to the poems of next week."[1] The military camaraderie and hard-edged critical unanimity of the New Critical method combined masculine physicality with scientific engineering to redeem poetry from any lingering whiff of sentimental femininity, not that Brooks and his men were teaching any of the three-named lady poets Hemingway had mocked. Understanding poetry was taught as a man's job, a triumph of reason over emotion.

But these days poetry has been dislodged from the center of the literary curriculum by fiction, drama, cultural studies, and even literary theory. Teachers lament that students find it difficult and intimidating. According to Anne Lake Prescott, in the US "even good students can arrive at college afraid of it, some because they think it a mystery into which they are not initiated and some because they take poems to be cryptic messages with nuggets of advice or belief – like a fortune cookie."[2] In the UK, writes Stephen Regan, debates over English and the national curriculum have ignored poetry as a distinct genre, so that "while the poetry festivals flourish, some undergraduate students are likely to arrive at university with little or no interest in poetry, confessing that they don't know how to read it and therefore can't be expected to understand or appreciate it."[3] Ann Thompson too remarks that "many students don't like poetry very much, and they particularly resist poetry that is difficult."

Yet many people commented on the spontaneous resurgence of poetry after September 11, 2001. United States poet laureate Billy Collins said, "In times of crisis, it's interesting that people don't turn to the novel . . . It's always poetry." In the *New York Times*, Dinitia Smith described the way "improvised memorials often conceived around poetry" sprung up around the city, and "poems flew through cyberspace across the country in e-mails from friend to friend" – Shelley's "Ozymandias," Auden's "September 1, 1939," Yeats's rough beast, Marianne Moore's "What Are Years?" Many ordinary people wrote poetry as well, some of it collected and reprinted by British Poet Laureate Andrew Motion: "Poetry is the form we turn to instinctively at moments of intensity, whether it be to celebrate or grieve. Why? Because of its compressions and distillations, its different perspectives, its meditative pace. Because of its link with our strongest emotions. Because of its power to console. Because of its separation (of whatever degree) from ordinary speech, which creates a sense of occasion. Because of its implicit demand to remember."[4]

The qualities of compression, mnemonics, emotion, and consolation in poetry provide some directions about how it might be a paradigm for active, student-centered teaching in the university as well as primary and secondary education. Collins argues that teaching poetry offers some fundamental cognitive and intellectual skills, and that reading a poem "replicates the way we learn and think." He sees many parallels between poetry and learning: "When we read a poem, we enter the consciousness of another. It requires that we loosen some of our fixed notions in order to accommodate another point of view . . . To follow the connections in a metaphor is to make a mental leap, to exercise an imaginative agility, even to open a new synapse as two disparate things are linked." Collins thinks of poetic form as "a way of thinking, an angle of approach," that helps students understand how information must be "shaped and contoured in order to be intelligible."[5]

Indeed, Robert Scholes (Brown) believes that English teachers, and especially the New Critics, are to blame for poetry's sad decline, and that the New Criticism was "bad for poets and poetry and really terrible for students and teachers of poetry." The "diminished status" of poetry, he argues, is as much the fault of "well-intentioned teachers" as reluctant and ignorant students. *Understanding Poetry* was one of the most influential textbooks ever published, but the Brooks-and-Warren approach to reading poems "had the effect of purging the curriculum of the very poems that had once functioned to give students textual pleasure, thus preparing them to take an interest in poetic texts that did not display their hearts so obviously on their poetic sleeve." Further, the New Critical approach hammered out by teachers at Yale and elsewhere emphasized a technical terminology of irony, paradox, tension, and symbolism which took precedence over human interests and feelings.

In order to restore poetry to a more central position in the literary curriculum, Scholes argues, "we must select from a fuller range of poetic texts, and we should present them in a way that encourages readers to connect the poems to their lives." He believes that "the poet's life and world are relevant."[6] In short, Collins and Scholes stress the accessibility of poetry rather than its difficulty, and encourage students to start with the poets and poems who are most directly meaningful to them, even when these are poets and poems despised by the New Critics and their pedagogic heirs: Edna St. Vincent Millay, or even Edgar Guest. Their idea is that with poetry, as with other genres, students must begin with the familiar and emotionally relevant, and move from there to more complex forms and historically-distant works.

Teaching Poetry and Learning Techniques

In teaching poetry, every instructor will need to call upon and combine a range of techniques and methods. Teaching an individual poet or a single poem involves different problems than organizing a whole course. Obviously, much depends on historical issues, and how familiar the language and reference and context of the poem will be to readers. But no one can argue that it is easier to teach the avant-garde L-A-N-G-U-A-G-E poets than Chaucer. The teacher has to ask herself about the intended audience of learners – beginners, advanced, majors, graduate students, dabblers, artists, scientists?

Ideally, whenever we teach, we will be steeped in the literature at hand, overflowing with ideas about how to present it. Realistically, however, we are often in the situation of the hypothetical teacher of shorter Elizabethan poetry, addressed by Patrick Cheney: "You are teaching a course . . . for the first time, you have not had adequate time to prepare it, and . . . you are anxiously searching for concrete advice. In other words, you are alone on the platform. The night is bitter cold, you are sick at heart, and you feel harrowed with fear and wonder. What follows aims to help you pass the minutes of this night: a . . . poetry survival kit."[7] Teaching methods are an all-purpose poetry survival kit.

1 Subject-centered methods

Poetics

The poetic territory immediately presents problems because it comes with a specialized technical language. Marjorie Perloff, who has written numerous books on experimental and avant-garde modern and contemporary poetry, defines poetry in terms that are "quite conventional and classical. I believe a poem differs from routine or normal discourse (like this statement, for instance) by being the art form that foregrounds language, in its complexity, intensity, and, especially, *relatedness* . . . In the poetic text, everything is related to everything else – or should be – the whole being a construct of sameness and difference in pleasing proportions."[8] Faculty have to decide how they will teach the subjects of poetics, metrics, and prosody. Jonathan Arac (Columbia) believes that "without attention to prosody, poetry may seem like arbitrary magic rather than a codified technology of verbal power."[9]

Diane Middlebrook taught her first poetry courses in 1966 – Introduction to Poetry (now the required course for majors at Stanford), and Poetry and Poetics. Talking about poetry, she believes, is about technique and formal history, so the texts can be from anyplace. On the level of course planning, she believes every course needs a throughline, to establish boundaries. She organizes the introductory course around four topics: narrative, lyric, satire, and image, as an efficient way to show how poetic language has been generated and renewed.

Middlebrook, a poet herself, sees students' resistance to learning poetics as the main disadvantage of teaching poetry. She believes that in order to understand the special nature of poetry, students have to grasp the almost platonic quality of poetic forms: "The challenge is to bring alive the idea that poetry exists in the abstract before it exists in particular. The most exciting moments come when the students get that. Poetry is written in a line of syllables with sonic and auditory relationships. The sonic patterns encode a set of meanings that are already there." Middlebrook assigns a textbook, M. H. Abrams's *Glossary of Literary Terms*, as background and insists that to understand poetry you need "a precise vocabulary." Nevertheless, she adds, "students need direct encounter with poetry, not just abstractions." "In teaching blank verse, for example, we look at Wyatt, Shakespeare, Wordsworth, and Wallace Stevens. The blank verse line is susceptible to variation by a strong poet. We look at the way the 10-syllable beat can be changed."[10]

Metaphors

Some teachers have used metaphors and themes to organize the reading of poetry. One very ingenious idea comes from Julia Reinhard Lupton (University of California, Irvine). Lupton uses the imagery of flowers to organize a course on Renaissance lyric: "A glance at the social life of flowers in the contemporary world can draw on your students' local knowledge as a resource for reading Renaissance poetry. The floral business depends on love and death . . . But while funeral flowers often remain attached to a living plant, the flowers of romance are almost always cut flowers, displaying that element of cultural refashioning that signals the frustration that gives sexual desire its special structure and urgency. (I also like to tell my students that potted plants make good gifts for Mother's Day but not for Valentines Day, and that receipt of a living plant from a boyfriend or girlfriend often indicates that the romance itself is dying.)" Lupton suggests that "the sexual and linguistic life of flowers offers a sensuous, immediately accessible center around which the potentialities of rhetorical, mythopoetic, and psychoanalytic criticism can blossom in any classroom."[11]

Genres

Heather Dubrow (University of Wisconsin) notes that genre criticism is sometimes identified with an older, outmoded approach to literature, but that she finds it a good way to teach poetry. In a course on sixteenth-century poetry, she tried organizing the semester in terms of genre. Even when genre is not at the center of the course, Dubrow tries to acknowledge the difficulty of literary form for undergraduates, and help them relate it to popular and social forms they already know.[12]

Stephen Regan suggests that "courses with a strong generic emphasis can be powerfully effective in opening up discussion of the poem in history. A carefully structured course on the sonnet can amply demonstrate the close relationship between eloquence and power . . . and it can also show how the sonnet flexibly accommodates a range of very different voices over several centuries: the radical, republican voices of John Milton and Tony Harrison, the anguished, confessional voices of George Herbert and Gerard Manley Hopkins, the intimate amatory voices of Elizabeth Barret Browning and Christina Rosssetti." He also suggests teaching a short course on the elegy, "juxtaposing 'Lycidas' with later works such as Auden's elegy 'In Memory of W. B. Yeats' and Heaney's 'The Strand at Lough Beg.'"[13] Roland Greene teaches the lyric. "How the genre developed makes a compelling object of study, describing a fairly strong literary-historical narrative, and drawing on the vantages of gender, institutions, politics, print, and religions."[14]

Background

We need to keep in mind that students outside of Stanford, Oxbridge, or the Ivies may need more subject-centered training before they can even think about prosody or metaphor. George Klawitter of St. Edward's University (Austin, Texas) believes that undergraduates need a detailed study guide and supplementary reading in order to understand and enjoy Milton. His study guide to Book 9 of *Paradise Lost* is designed to be "sequential . . . no question anticipates material that comes later. It makes no sense to ask students how Pandemonium contrasts with heaven until students reach a description of heaven." His six-question study guide, and handouts, for Book 9 asks students to take up issues of tone, biblical creation sources, gender, dialog, and genre with reference to specific passages and lines.[15]

Michael M. Levy, who teaches at the University of Wisconsin, Stout, describes his students as "lacking virtually all the extensive, historical, literary, mythological, and theological information necessary to even a partial understanding of the poem." He tries to give them some historical and biographical background, in part because "they honestly do not understand why anyone would want to write a poem."[16]

2 Teacher-centered methods

Reading aloud

A dramatically-effective method of teaching poetry is reading it aloud. Hugh Kenner (Johns Hopkins) is a believer in the physical properties of the poem. He recalls with affection a student who had learned to recite poetry from her father, and knew "The Ancient Mariner" by heart before she could talk. She was a wonderful student, because "she needed no persuasion, notably, about poetry's ancient mnemonic function." But rather than having his own students memorize, Kenner reads the poem aloud himself "with force propelled by a heritage of Welsh preachers. Whatever I'm teaching, 'The Sunne Rising,' or 'Canto XX,' or *Ulysses*, I do much reading aloud. Whether it is exemplary reading or not Sir Laurence Olivier might well dispute; but it does have two advantages. It slows down the pace at which the students encounter the words. And it nudges them, continually, from eye to ear. Maybe even, they parody me in the dorms. If so, they're beginning to vocalize." Only after students have listened to the poem does Kenner move to close reading.[17]

Camille Paglia's favorite teacher at SUNY-Binghamton, Milton Kessler, read poetry aloud "making great use of dynamics, another of the losses rock music has suffered since the Sixties. Like the blues shouters, Kessler could roar, then drop off to a rasp or whisper. Poetry was music-drama. I recently learned that Kessler had studied voice and opera as a young man and had even been a spear carrier at the old Met."[18]

Whether or not they can claim a genealogy of Welsh preachers or experience as spear-carriers, many teachers see reading aloud as an important step in teaching poetry. The medievalist Donald Howard was keen on having the professor read many passages of Chaucer aloud, even if he is "hopelessly without histrionic ability." But having students attempt to read, he thinks, is "embarrassing to the reader and boring to all."[19]

Lecturing

Teaching a poem for the first time, Diane Middlebrook will plan three lectures: technique, trope, and emotion. The lecture is an effort to make the text choices "illustrative of the way that emotional and cultural intelligence is transmitted in the poem." Middlebrook considers T. S. Eliot's "The Love Song of J. Alfred Prufrock" the "most important poem for captivating students, for reaching them where they live." She begins by stressing a detached question of genre and literary history – the poem as a dramatic monologue, descending from Browning. Engagement with the author comes later. Understanding the techniques of the dramatic monologue points up the way the poem works against the "identification with the lyric 'I'." Middlebrook also "pulls out the pronoun moments" and emphasizes the role of the implied listener: " 'Let us go then, you and I.' Who is the 'you?' " An answer lies within the poem, and by the end of the process, Middlebrook hopes students will see that the fragmented subjectivity of the narrator makes You and I both parts of himself. By the ending – "Human voices wake us and we drown" – I and you can come together.

She always emphasizes the beginning and the ending of poems, "because the poem is circular, and requires understanding of opening and closure." Second, she looks at allusions. What is Hamlet doing in the poem? Since most students will recognize the allusion, they are allowed "to discover that they already know something about Prufrock from their literary education."

3 Student-centered methods

Lecturers can present, explain, and demonstrate the subject matter of poetic analysis and interpretation, but telling the students about it is not the same as involving them in it. Poetry is well suited to the active classroom,

Diane Middlebrook thinks, because "it's not like anything else. In poetry you read everything, including the punctuation. Everything is an inexhaustible site of reading and interpretation. It's not just something you can learn on your own; poetry is best consumed in public. We need to hear other people talking about it. Even a professor might impose too swift a closure on meaning without a student's fabulous intervention. And two equally plausible interpretations can exist together." The potential power of teaching poetry depends on active student engagement with both poetic language and meaning.

Memorizing

The oldest pedagogical method for teaching poetry is memorization. Many of us will recall having to learn poems by heart in elementary school or high school, or memorizing lines and poems voluntarily. I still can recite several of Shakespeare's sonnets, Arnold's "Dover Beach," and Browning's "My Last Duchess," along with a great deal of less reputable and politically-incorrect verse including Robert Service and Vachel Lindsay's "The Congo." Knowing poems by heart was once the sign and the pride of an educated person. Now that skill is disappearing. Having students memorize poems seems like a rote exercise, more suitable for the schoolmarm than the professor, and out of place in the modern classroom.

Yet both poets and distinguished teachers of poetry still recommend memorization as a useful pedagogical tool. The great academic champion of poetic memorization in our time is Harold Bloom. As he recalls, "as a boy of eight, I would walk about chanting Housman's and William Blake's lyrics to myself, and I still do, less frequently yet with undiminished fervor." Bloom sees memorization as the first significant step in reading poems. "Silent intensive rereadings of a shorter poem that truly *finds* you should be followed by recitations to yourself, until you discover that you are in possession of the poem."[20] Before he gets to detailed analysis, Bloom emphasizes what he calls "possession-by-memory," the poem's accessibility to memorization, because of its relative brevity and its internal mnemonic devices. Once committed to memory, he believes, the poem has the capacity to induce a sense of trancendence in the reader who recites it. "I know many people," he concludes, "who continually recite poems to themselves in the awareness that the possession of the poem helps them to live their lives."[21]

Alice Quinn, the poetry editor of the *New Yorker*, agrees. Quinn explains that "memorizing allows you to experience language, to experience privacy. When you are memorizing poems, you are in an intimate connection with the person who made them. It is a profound source of spiritual nourishment." In her courses on poetry at Columbia University, she told a reporter, "she makes all her students memorize poems, an experience, she says, in an age when memorization is frowned upon, that irrevocably changes them. It is no accident, she says, that most poets who teach insist on the students being able to recite poems from memory. 'It gives them a great sense of how the thing is made, the sounds, how the words are chiming, a great sense of the current of the thought and the beautiful labor poems achieve.' "[22]

Billy Collins is another strong advocate of memorization. "Anyone who has taken a poetry course with me," he writes, "knows that I am big on memorization." Why memorize? Because, he explains, "to memorize is not only to possess something . . . It is to make what is memorized an almost physical part of us, to turn it into a companion." Poetry is especially suited for this because "it began as a memory system. Mnemosyne was, by Zeus, the mother of all the Muses. In poetry's most ancient form, the now-familiar features of rhyme, meter, repletion, alliteration and the like were simply mnemonic devices – tricks to facilitate the storage and retrieval of information, and vital information at that." In his utopian university, all students would recite a few lines from a poem as they receive their degrees.[23]

Recitation

In Diane Middlebrook's classes, the students read the poem aloud. Middle-brook believes there is a correct way to read poetry: "The line ending is a marker and a pause the ear must note. Both syntactical units and the line ending must be stressed, so that the ear can distinguish between syntactic and structural units. Denise Levertov calls the unpunctuated line ending 'half a comma.' That enjambment is important. Moreover, the reader of a poem is not an actor but a musical instrument. Students can interpret, yes, but they need also to show the melody. Poetic and emotional stresses fall in different places. I tell the students to read poems into a tape recorder for practice."[24]

Even in the course on political poetry I have discussed in chapter 2, where he determines the intellectual agenda, Cary Nelson has his students read or chant the poems in chorus. "We did a lot of oral performing of poetry," he notes; and "choral classroom readings . . . worked extraordinarily well for some of the sound poems of the 1920s . . . Reading them aloud in class – sometimes in unison and sometimes contrapuntally – students discovered uncanny power and humor in texts that had previously seemed meaning-less." But he had to admit defeat in his effort "to win some sympathy for the most blatantly pro-Soviet revolutionary poems of the early 1930s . . . I can still remember the dull, flat sound of thirty-five students unenthusiasti-cally reading the line 'All Power to the Soviets' from Sol Funaroff's 'What the Thunder Said: A Fire Sermon.' "[25] However grim this moment, it was better for the students to read the line than having to meet it mute on the page, or hear the professor proclaim it.

The commonplace book

During a period in which many teachers besides Nelson, especially those who are teaching women poets before the nineteenth century, are challenging the poetic canon enshrined in anthologies, canon formation will be a lively classroom topic. Many teachers of poetry require students to assemble a commonplace book, or personal anthology, in which they record their own favorite lines and verses from the period, with an introduction that explains their principles of selection. Diana E. Henderson (MIT) asks her "students to compose their own commonplace books, handwritten rather than typed, in which they may include their meditations, verse, and illustrations, as well as passages they found memorable in our reading."[26] Caroline McManus (California State University at Los Angeles) has her students organize their commonplace books topically. In a Renaissance poetry course, she may have them adopt the categories from Robert Allott's *Englands Parnassus*: "Art, Beautie, Chastitie, Death, Despaire, Gifts, God, Greatnes, Heart, Honour, Jealouzie, Kisses, Lechery, Love, Marriage, Nature, Night, Pride, Princes, Sleepe, Teares, Time, Treason, and Venus." At the end of the course, students select one of these topics for a term paper.[27]

Clark Hulse recommends using the Web for this purpose: "The Web creates an easy way for students to make their own commonplace books simply by browsing, cutting, and pasting at a Web site . . . Students creating such personal anthologies should be encouraged to rework the material thoroughly – by arranging and juxtaposing, throwing in significant visual material, retitling poems, writing short linking commentaries or fictional biographical vignettes, or even rewriting the poems themselves as it is necessary, useful, or desirable."[28]

Writing poetry

Should a course on poetry also be a course on creative writing? Now that creative writing programs flourish at most campuses, the art of composing poetry has been detached from the history, understanding, and analysis of poetic language. But many teachers maintain that even a brief personal struggle with the Muse, and with the structures and strictures of poetic form, is one of the most useful ways to learn to read poetry. According to Frank Kermode, "it can still be argued that people who have actually written Petrarchan sonnets, villanelles, sestinas, ballades, and so forth, whatever the merit of their performances, actually understand more about poetry than people who haven't, and may have a better understanding of more modern, less

71

communicable, technical achievements . . . I have encountered, in a graduate literature class, students who have been taught to write poems as a major part of their studies. Belatedly, I am almost convinced that this is where the study of literature ought to begin."[29]

More specifically, Scholes recommends spending a lot of time in a course on a single poet whose work covers a wide range of styles and subjects, whose tone varies from the harsh to the tragic – perhaps Robert Herrick. He thinks students should also be encouraged to imitate the poet's forms, from brief epigrams to sonnets and so on.

But whether or not the study of poetry ought to begin with writing it, writing poetry can be an illuminating and memorably hands-on part of a course. Caroline McManus asks students to write a sonnet. "With the experience of composition comes humility and less dismissiveness of the sixteenth-century sonneteers' achievements."[30] Diane Middlebrook gives her students an assignment to write a sonnet on a classic trope, such as "the hunter hunted." Heather Dubrow points out that "writing assignments that involve actually composing a text in a genre, though difficult and upsetting for some students, prove stimulating for others." She has been successful in encouraging her students to "think about that genre by simply creating a couplet."[31]

McManus also types up all the student writing, and circulates it to the class without names – a technique that reinforces their involvement in the assignment, but a bit tricky, because sometimes students are embarrassed by having their efforts made public and exposed to criticism, even under conditions of anonymity. If you are going to circulate student writing, you need to make it clear to the students at the start of the course.

Parody is an excellent method of teaching as well. Kristine Haugen, teaching "Rape of the Lock," had students in groups of four "come up with their own mock epics. I said they had to include a hero, a villain, a conflict and resolution (i.e. a plot), at least two symbols freighted with extreme poetic significance, divine 'machinery' and the name of a muse they would invoke. The subjects they chose showed that if nothing else, they'd gotten the point from Pope that making a mock epic usually involves applying epic tropes to familiar settings." In a Chaucer course, a student "brought in some video footage of the Princeton Triangle Club's skit called 'W.O.B. seeks S.W.M.' It began with a red-headed, gap-toothed mama signing up for a video-dating service and introducing herself as 'Bath, Wife of.' The sales assistant then springs to her feet and with fanatic awe and says, 'Not *the* Wife of Bath – proto-feminist icon?' Then the Wife launches into a song-and-dance number, half in middle-English, for which she is joined by three guys dressed as the Pardoner, the Parson, and the Cook. After much laughter and merriment had by all, we launched into questions from the students and myself, such as 'Is the Wyf a feminist?' and 'How do we define feminist?'"

Writing about poetry – the portfolio

John Webster (University of Washington) has his students keep a portfolio of their writing on poems throughout the term, breaking down the writing assignments into blocks geared to "helping less-experienced readers develop a method for first noticing and then exploring poetic language. With my prompts, I try to break the process of reading into discrete steps: early in the quarter the tasks run heavily toward locating effects to explore; later I ask for more sustained exploration and argumentation. I follow the same principle in individual units as well. When I teach sonnets, for example, though my large-scale goal will be to leave students able to develop readings of sonnets as compressed, miniaturized plays, each with characters, a dramatic situation, and a plot, my first prompt is very simple . . . for their first response paper, I only ask that they notice and explore three to five words that seem to have a special role in the poem."

"Students also benefit greatly from the portfolio's providing a concrete place in which they can see their own work grow. This is true literally; by course end students will have accumulated thirty to forty pages of writing about Elizabethan poetry, all of it produced by their own hands. But the sense of a student's work growing has a more abstract force, for as students review their work to write the self-reflexive essay, they can see for themselves how much more sophisticated their thinking has become."[32]

Comparison and contrast

One of the most effective ways to show students how poetic language works is to have them compare a poem with a prose statement of the same theme, or compare two or more poems on similar themes. Roland Greene "might take a short poem and put it alongside a suggestive English or other prose text from the period, observing how the two texts elucidate each other, and then compare the same poem with a roughly similar poem from a contemporaneous continental or American society."[33]

Jonathan Arac regularly uses comparison to teach poetic structure: "We read Johnson's 'On the Death of Dr. Robert Levet.' Juxtaposing this work with Gray [sonnet on the death of Richard West and 'A Slumber Did My Spirit Seal'], we stage a fruitful comparison of three poems of mourning from a fifty-year period. We begin by noting in the three poems the very different emphases between focus on the speaker (almost total in Gray) and focus on the deceased (almost total in Johnson). Wordsworth might then seem to reconcile the extremes of his two predecessors, but in his poem students usually find, frustratingly, less of the detail they value about either speaker or deceased. I then change this line of discussion by asking the question 'Which would you prefer to have as your memorial?' Students are often surprised to discover that they prefer Johnson."[34]

I have found it effective to begin classes on Emily Dickinson by having students compare versions of her poems as they appeared in anthologies pre-1960, with all the idiosyncracies of diction, imagery, and punctuation edited out, and in the definitive edition taken from manuscripts. Here, for example, are the two versions of the third stanza of one poem:

The Chariot	712
We passed the school where children played, Their lessons scarcely done; We passed the fields of gazing grain, We passed the setting sun.	We passed the School where Children strove At Recess-in-the-Ring- We passed the Fields of Gazing Grain- We passed the Setting Sun-

Having students note the differences between the two versions, and then try to account for them is a good way for them both to understand Dickinson's uniqueness and also see how that uniqueness violated expectations of women's poetic composition. Such an exercise also provides opportunities for arguments about taste and value.

Working from what students already know

Many teachers invite students to use lyrics of popular songs as a way of getting started on poetic language; some textbooks and handbooks actually include lyrics like Bob Dylan's "Highway 61 Revisited," and invite students to compare it to poems like Yeats's "Easter 1916."

Kristine Haugen uses astrology and horoscopes as a way of illustrating beliefs in determinism and destiny. "A few tried to deny that they ever read horoscopes in the paper; others gleefully admitted it, and they chatted about who was what sign. I pointed out that modern astrologers don't predict only events on the basis of your sign, they also predict your personality or innate characteristics on the basis of it. We applied this distinction of personality and event first back to *Paradise Lost*, and then back to 'The Nun's Priest's Tale,' where the rooster is deceived because of his urbanity, which is probably innate to roosters."

Irene Tayler has a different problem teaching Blake at MIT, where students are brilliant scientists, studying humanities, and Romantic poetry, only as a supplement to their core work in mathematics or engineering. She sees Blake as a "system builder" who especially appeals to these young thinkers. Her teaching methods stress the visual and analytical before the historical and aesthetic. Tayler gives an introductory lecture on Blake as a poet and artist; her first assignment is for students to describe in as much detail as they can the characteristics of a single plate from *Songs of Innocence*. In the next class, she puts up a slide of the plate, and all compare what they have seen. The effect, she says, "is electrifying. These students are trained observers who pride themselves on scientific accuracy and meticulous attention to detail. But each has seen some minute particular that the others have not, and the resulting experience is at once humbling to each and exhilarating to all. They are learning a new way to see, and from my point of view the less they know about Blake the better, for most of them having their first adult experience of struggling to understand in the absence of a preformulated system." Only after discussing the plate do they turn to the text, which further complicates the act of interpretation. Tayler then repeats the process with *Songs of Experience*.[35]

Putting It All Together: Some Examples

No teacher ever uses one method alone. In planning and teaching a poetry course, a professor will draw on many techniques, but the best course will include more active than teacher-centered methods. Feminist critic Sandra Gilbert, co-author of *The Madwoman in the Attic*, is also a poet. Gilbert is an eloquent, erudite, and very funny lecturer; we co-taught an undergraduate lecture course on women's writing at Princeton in the 1980s, and I learned a lot from the way she combined personal stories with literary history, film clips with close readings, biography with prosody. In her discussion classes on Sylvia Plath, she combines a feminist intellectual framework with careful attention to the conventions and techniques of the verse. Explaining the way she teaches Plath's "Daddy," about which she has written in many contexts, Gilbert confesses that her first obstacle is the poem's familiarity to her, and she has developed techniques for breaking through her own "preconceived and carefully worked out interpretations" without straying into "eccentric meditations on particular points that continue to puzzle me." In other words, like many of us, Gilbert tries to avoid either the glib and canned overview, or the hyperspecialized and arcane detail.

She is concerned about having Plath's poetry overwhelmed by "the invasion of the aesthetic by the biographical." In order to have students concentrate on the text, she reads it aloud. Gilbert then tries to get them

75

"to say as much as they can about what they think the text itself means and as much as possible about how it works, how it sounds, how it feels. If necessary, I go around the room, or the table, asking people to mention particular aspects of the poem that interest them and that they would especially like to consider."

I have mentioned that the most important part of a discussion class is the opening question; Gilbert asks "who the speaker is and what her 'problem' is – a question that may seem simple but one that opens out, obviously, into many larger issues." She follows up on the poem's Holocaust and vampire imagery, its slanginess, its mythic elements. One resolution of these contradictions for students, Gilbert suggests, would be to relate "Daddy" to issues of modernism and postmodernism; but she finds this an appropriate point to introduce biographical, historical, and social questions, to ask what it meant "to be a woman, born in America in 1932, reading major poetry and trying to write major poetry in the years from 1952 to 1963?" Gilbert goes on to organize Plath's poetry in terms of relationships to the male literary tradition and confrontations with a female ancestry – the "disquieting muses." Sharing details of manuscript drafts of "Daddy," "Lady Lazarus," and "Medusa" with students, Gilbert points out Plath's "careful revisions" to show how the poet moved from emotion to craft.[36]

Jewel Spears Brooker (Eckerd College) teaches *The Waste Land* in a course for freshmen and sophomores. Her approach is to focus on the theme of failed love in the poem, in three carefully-planned 90-minute class periods. For the first, Brooker assigns the entire poem. In her lecture, she offers a close reading of the epigraph and first seven lines of the poem, and provides students with a detailed account of its mythic and literary sources, linking them to the "relation between love and fruitfulness, between lovelessness and waste, in the myths of Frazer and Weston, in the Bible, and in a few well-known works in the Western tradition."

Then Brooker moves to a more student-centered approach to learning. In preparation for the second class, students reread the poem, dividing it into "nuggets of narrative or drama or song." They also pair off and practice reading three dramatic fragments aloud: lines 77–138, 139–72, and 215–56 – "scenes of love in the modern world." In class, students volunteer or are invited to take the dramatic roles in presenting these sections of the poem, and Brooker's role is "chiefly one of organizing the reading and encouraging discussion afterward;" she asks "a few leading questions about failed love and waste lands."

For the final meeting, students apply what they have learned; they write an essay showing how other sections of the poem are relevant to the theme of waste lands and their causes. In class, they share their ideas; and Brooker finds that they not only "have definite ideas on the poem," but often have memorized some lines. In her conclusion, she stresses the moral and personal values of literary reconstruction: "In taking fragments strewn on the surface of the poem and re-collecting them (both remembering where they came from and gathering them up again), we and our students are shoring up our ruins in a collaborative life-enhancing act."[37]

For teachers, comparing two expert approaches to the same course is a useful way to think about theories and methods. The late Donald Howard, for example, could imagine a perfect Chaucer course, which would last a year, include all the work, and effortlessly initiate students into Middle English and the medieval world view. But in reality, he admits, students will read *The Canterbury Tales*, if anything. And if teachers of Chaucer disagree on methods, they must agree on goals: "To put the student in touch with the mind of Geoffrey Chaucer."

Howard's ideas on method are primarily teacher-centered. He begins with the "General Prologue" and the "Knight's Tale" – the prologue because it establishes the whole, the tale because it is the high-minded template of romantic ideals against which the rest must resonate. But Howard also points out obstacles in this process. The prologue is always heavily footnoted, and he advises students to skip most of the annotation and read for meaning. The tale is beyond students' linguistic expertise, and Howard lets them read it in a normalized-spelling version. Indeed, he believes that Chaucerians often make a fetish of Middle English scribal spelling, and that it just gets in the way of student enjoyment and apprehension.

Once launched, Howard thinks, it's just a matter of deciding "what order to put the tales in." He prefers the Ellesmere order of the tales in which the 'Nun's Priest's Tale' comes last, because "it is the hardest tale to teach." Indeed, Howard felt that he himself had never taught it with complete success; "to understand it, one must know all those features: courtly love, rhetoric, Geoffrey of Vinsauf on the death of Richard I, medicine, astrology, dreams – you name it. The poor teacher must struggle to explain all this background, and nothing spoils a joke more than explaining it."

Howard's view of the best classroom practice is to lecture, and let the students ask occasional questions. "It is one of the pieties of our profession," he writes, "that a good teacher, instead of 'lecturing away,' gets students to speak their thoughts. But Chaucer does not in my experience lend himself to the discussion method; his age is too distant from ours, there are too many facts to be learned, the language presents too many difficulties."[38]

But John Fleming (Princeton) disagrees with many of Howard's ideas. "To omit 'Troilus and Criseyde,' Chaucer's one perfect ambitious poem and one of the best in our literature, is a shame. Highly motivated students –

and there is an important index of self-selection among students who elect Chaucer courses – can do both most of the 'Canterbury Tales' and all of 'Troilus' in a semester. Obviously two semesters would be better in principle. Howard is right about not worrying too much about orthography, but in practical fact there is no 'modern' edition of Chaucer that limits itself to mere spelling. And the difference between reading Chaucer in Middle English and reading him in modern translation is the difference between taking a bath and taking a bath with one's socks on."

Fleming also believes that having students read Chaucer aloud is important: "It allows students to 'own' the poetry. Learning passable Middle English pronunciation is also a finite task that almost every student can do, and with its achievement comes a feeling of power. But above all Chaucer is a poet of sounds par excellence – you really do need to speak and hear him. Students can see for themselves the 'modernity' in Chaucer. They need help in understanding its alterity. And the real excitement for teacher and student alike is the exploration of the dialogue between the two."[39]

Overall, the models for teaching poetry – performance, imitation, generic focus, comparison, connection, engagement, evaluation – are traditionally the most hands-on in the literary repertoire. For these reasons, thinking about poetry is a good place to start thinking about teaching literature in general.

Chapter 5
Teaching Drama

It's a dirty job teaching Shakespeare. But somebody's got to do it.
  Edward Pechter, Shakespeare Quarterly *41 (Summer 1990): 173*

In a way, my relationship with Shakespeare has been the most lasting and stable
one I've ever had with a man.
  Gayle Greene, "Looking at History," Changing Subjects, *9*

Teaching drama is also a paradigm for active learning and the reflective teaching of literature, because teaching is itself a dramatic art and it takes place in a dramatic setting. As Kenneth Eble points out, "it is commonly forgotten that the classroom offers the rudiments of a stage. In auditoriums, used as classrooms, everything is there, including curtains and lights. There is little to be lost and much to be gained in using the classroom, when appropriate, as theater."[1] The professor is also an actor, with teaching assistants as the supporting cast, and students as the audience. The classroom space with its entrances and exits, the teaching hour with its rhythms of exposition and climax, relate to the theater and illuminate the theatrical experience.

For a teacher of dramatic literature, the theatrical metaphor is reflected in the structure of the learning experience; and we waste much of our potential if we do not take advantage of these parallels. But many teachers ignore them. Richard Bausch, for instance, writes: "When I teach sophomore literature, before I give any other assignments, I ask my students to do an annotated bibliography about *Hamlet*. They must find ten critical essays about the play, read them, and then summarize for me, merely to show that they have indeed read the essays. This is less to teach them about *Hamlet* than to expose them to the ways and means of critical speech about that great play, and, by extension, about any other work of literature."[2] Bausch's intention is to shake students out of their complacency about finding any single key to the play. But such an assignment risks alienating and intimidating students as well.

Intellectually as well as pedagogically, exploring the connections and contradictions of page and stage is part of the most up-to-date thinking in the field. According to J. L. Styan of Northwestern, author of the influential book *The Dramatic Experience* (1965), "for an influential number of instructors who are devoted to teaching drama, the great advance since about mid-century has been recognition of it as a performing art."[3] This approach has been most highly developed and theorized with regard to Shakespeare. It was initiated in the 1960s, by Homer (Murph) Swander, who organized a radical and influential MLA session on teaching through acting workshops, and developed through the work of such scholars as Bernard Beckermann, who taught an NEH summer institute at Folger Library in 1982 on teaching drama through performance, Lois Potter of the University of Delaware, who directed a yearlong institute at the Folger Library in 1992–3 called "Shakespeare and the Languages of Performance," Alan and Cynthia Dessen at the University of North Carolina, who lead a group called ACTER, and Miriam Gilbert of the University of Iowa, who has directed several NEH Summer Seminars on performance for high school and college teachers. An essential tool for this approach is John Barton's *Playing Shakespeare*, a book based on a series of televised workshops with actors from the Royal Shakespeare Company, accompanied by videotapes. The *Shakespeare Quarterly*, under the editorship of Ralph Alan Cohen, devoted three special issues, in 1974, 1984, and 1990, exclusively to teaching, and they show that performance studies came to dominate the field of pedagogy in the 1980s and had become institutionalized by the 1990s. Nevertheless, I suspect that many teachers of literature outside of the Shakespearean field are unfamiliar with it, and with its implications for the teaching of drama in general, as well as for other literary genres.

Teaching Shakespeare through Performance, part of the "Options for Teaching" series of the MLA, is an excellent introduction to this field. All the contributors to this volume emphasize the ways that classroom space is theatrical space, and the manifold ways that students learn by performing Shakespeare. James N. Loehlin explains that "teachers of Shakespeare have a unique opportunity to involve their students directly in the material being studied. Math students can reconstruct the proofs of their predecessors, art history students can copy a Vermeer – but students of Shakespearean drama can actually create the thing they study. By becoming themselves involved in the complex interaction of text, actors, and audience that constitutes a play in performance, students can gain unique insights into Shakespearean drama and the Elizabethan theatrical culture that produced it."[4] As the editor, Milla Cozart Riggio, explains, "performance initially may seem to imply only one approach to teaching drama. But this book is based on the premise that performance pedagogy – more than simply an approach or an option – provides a holistic frame with a broad range of options and implications."[5] Riggio defines performance teaching to include full student theatrical productions, reading scenes in classroom workshops, using films and videos, attending live productions, studying the stage history of the plays, and above all, involving teachers and students together in dramatic interpretations of character, structure, and action.

David Bevington and Gavin Witt, at the University of Chicago, collaborate in teaching a course that uses their expertise as scholar and dramaturg. They ask "Why use acting or dramatic-reading workshops in literature-oriented classes in Shakespeare? The proposition may strike some teachers as a contradiction in terms. Acting workshops belong in a theater department, some might argue; literature professors teach literature. Our graduate English departments generally do not teach acting or offer instruction on how to teach an acting class; for literature teachers to attempt such a thing smacks of amateurism and of poaching on others' terrain in the war-torn landscape of the academy. Most teachers of literature have little or no experience even as semiprofessional actors; will they not look foolish in front of their students if they undertake to be knowledgeable about the practical aspects of theater production?" Why spend time in class acting when you could be analyzing and criticizing and mastering all the theoretical approaches? They argue that the great virtue of an acting approach is that it is "interactive. It gets students involved, gets them speaking, talking, and on their feet when scenes are blocked out . . . workshop teaching is an effective way to bring drama to life in the classroom."

Bevington and Witt used acting workshops as a voluntary supplement to the course as a whole, but they also incorporated aspects of it into the lectures themselves. Understanding the importance of beginnings, on the first day of class, for example, they began not with announcements, but by having Witt deliver Hamlet's Act II soliloquy, "O, what a rogue and peasant slave am I," and then asking students to respond on the basis of watching and hearing the performance. "Through the use of this soliloquy as an opening gambit, we undertook to put the class on notice that, for the following weeks, 'the play [was] the thing.'" The results were exciting; "our experience was that when students are asked to read aloud portions of the play and whenever possible to undertake rough stagings of a scene, the process opens up features undreamed of in silent, solitary perusal of the page."[6]

How should others begin to carry out such a drastically different method? Michael Shapiro, who attended the Beckermann seminar in 1982, recalls that he and the other participants "learned how to prepare students to do scene work in the classroom by doing it ourselves, as well as how to make pedagogic use of such work, and how to integrate performance-oriented teaching into drama courses."[7] Ideally, such seminars should be part of the graduate literature teacher-training program. Shapiro also describes improvisational techniques that teachers could adapt for their own classrooms.

The range of examples of performance teaching and its transformational effects is impressive. Michael O'Neill, at Oklahoma State University, for example, says that "Performance techniques desanctify Shakespeare in more practical ways than do, for instance, politically correct readings. Most analyses, however iconoclastic, encourage submission to the dominant critical-authorial voice and to the pressure of the thesis. Self-generated performance lets the students define their own Shakespeare in terms of the culture they live in."[8]

Most important from my point of view is that performance teaching provides a model of active engagement for the student of literature that we can use as a base for thinking about teaching other genres and topics. I have seen it done brilliantly in the classroom for all kinds of dramatic literature. At Gettysburg College, students presented a scene from *Medea* in the style of *The Godfather*, an apt parallel to Jason's high-handedness, enriched and expanded by the teacher's use of different translations of the play, and glosses on the Greek original.

In my own classes, I use video clips for *Hedda Gabler*, *A Doll House*, and *Miss Julie*. I've also invited professional actors to the class to discuss the videos with us. But Lois Potter (Delaware) worries that using videos and films may "confirm the group in its habits of passivity, especially if one turns out the lights during the show . . . unless trained to read films in their own right, the students are still in the position of passive consumers, evaluating and adjudicating among other people's interpretations, rather than evolving their own." She recommends playing a video of scene but avoiding the "pitfall of passive viewing," by showing it "after the class has itself experimented with ways of playing that scene."[9]

Potter points out that if "lecturing itself establishes teacher and students in the roles of performer and audience, lecturing about performance can be a double reinforcement of these roles." Nonetheless, she has been inspired by performance to risk more of it herself: "The more you watch other performers work in the classroom, the more you begin to see how to make students, and yourself, comfortable with the idea of acting. How much ability you yourself have does not matter." She offers reassurance and advice to the timid and untheatrical: "If you are a lively, outgoing person, it is easier to inspire confidence. But if you are not, there is a solution: plan everything very carefully, thinking at each stage about the worst case scenario and how you will deal with it. Then, once you start, try to enjoy everything. The experience of acting is so intense for all participants that it will make you and your mistakes less visible than usual." Finally, Potter has students come to her office for a "minirehearsal" of their assigned scene, really as a way to get students to come to see her informally, and to get to know them as individuals.[10]

Ralph Alan Cohen outlines his approach to the first scene of *King Lear*, which examines where characters enter, in what order, and when Kent begins to speak his lines. This focus, Cohen explains, means the students need to be familiar with the physical arrangement of the Elizabethan stage, and also to consider Elizabethan hierarchy. Cohen also discusses the importance of visible audience in Shakespeare and ways of helping students understand it. "The Elizabethan stage worked like a classroom in which the audience simultaneously experienced the subject and learned lessons about it. For that reason, teachers who stage their classrooms as Elizabethan theaters will not only find a place from which to view Shakespeare's language more clearly, they will also re-create a venue that teaches as it moves its audience."[11]

Performance teaching also works well with gender theory, Stephen Orgel explains: "In the classroom at Stanford University, where I teach a range of English majors and nonmajors, I have found discussions of performance practice the most helpful way of introducing undergraduates to the rarefied world of postmodern gender theory." In *As You Like It, Twelfth Night*, even *The Merchant of Venice*, reminding students that boys were playing the women's parts illuminates gender issues. In a class of about a hundred undergraduates, meeting for two 90-minute lectures and one discussion section a week, Orgel studies six plays in a nine-week semester. He spends a lot of time lecturing on stage history, and devotes about a third of each lecture to film clips, including clips from several versions of *Twelfth Night* to "analyze how the actress playing Viola conveys that, disguised as Cesario, she is a boy."[12]

Jill L. Levenson at Trinity College, University of Toronto, finds tracking the stage history of a single play an effective teaching method. For *Romeo and Juliet*, for example, her students examine productions from David Garrick's at Drury Lane in 1748, to Baz Luhrmann's film. In short, performance teaching offers flexibility and depth. Edward L. Rocklin defends its intellectual and academic rigor: "Readers may wonder whether I do not have an idealized view of our students, perceiving them not only as developing readers and apprentice writers but even as artists – if not quite potential Shakespeares. My reply is that to make a performance model work, you have only to believe that asking students to act as if they are artists will make them exercise their creativity . . . What we should be aiming for is a model of an English course in which the creative and the interpretive functions are fully integrated."[13]

At Princeton, Oliver Arnold, Larry Danson and Michael Cadden – faculty from different critical backgrounds who teach dramatic literature – agree on the importance of stressing performance, but with varying degrees of personal involvement. Oliver Arnold is a New Historian who trained with Stephen Greenblatt at Berkeley. In the classroom, however, he also asks whether a text is "a record of performance, and how to make plays first created as writing into performance. Even at Princeton, there is a huge divide in students' experience. Many students have seen lots of live theater and others have seen none. It certainly helps if students have some experience of theater so that they can understand its power."

Arnold himself believes that "as scholars, we have an affinity for a certain form. I felt powerfully that although I loved novels I wasn't good at writing about them, and I felt an affinity for thinking and writing about drama, that is partly connected to the challenges of teaching a form. At this stage, I think literary pleasure can be taught and conveyed. Like my teachers, I try to emphasize the fun of even rigorous analytic thinking about literature – it's always pleasurable." Arnold asks himself "what students need to know about the context that would make the play richer, more intelligible. How are larger bites of the play intersected?"[14]

Shakespearian scholar Larry Danson is most concerned as a scholar with the language of the play, but he points out that "the difference between teaching a novel and teaching a play is that students have to be active in supplying the thing the novel supplies for them. The novel will tell them 'he said angrily.' But so much of the drama has to be supplied. You have to help them think of a play not just as a book but as a script for a possible performance."[15]

Michael Cadden, who teaches drama in the English Department and chairs the Program in Theater and Dance, was trained at the Yale School of Drama. He is the most concerned with performance: "Plays are not meant to be read. If you see them in the theater, many decisions will have been made through the rehearsal process, but no matter how good a reader a student is, it is extremely hard to imagine the performative possibilities of the text. So my role as a teacher is to bring out what's on the page, and help them to set up and provide that performative supplement for themselves. They have to be active, the designer, the director, all the collaborators who make up the theatrical event. But potentially it's more exciting than teaching a novel or poem. For students, studying drama can be like discovering a whole new world."[16]

Arnold never tries to act himself, although he believes that "it's important to have students act things out. Students need the reminder of what a peculiar endeavor acting is – theater is an art form that depends on human beings as its representatives." He can "perform spontaneously – but then in the event it doesn't feel like performance, but like rediscovery." Often, he team-teaches Shakespeare with another instructor – "we have mutual levels of anxiety." Depending on his partner, he feels more or less cast in an audience role. With a "kinetic and energetic" colleague, I can "feel quite staid. With Michael Cadden, one guy is the stage guy and one the page guy."

Danson is a celebrated performer. "I'm not an actor, but I'm a ham, my students tell me, and I think a certain degree of modeling, both in lecture and in small groups, is helpful. I perform to the extent that I am asked every year whether I am a frustrated actor. I have got a pat answer to that now. I say, 'No, I'm not a frustrated actor; I'm a frustrated teacher.' I don't formally act things out. I have too great respect for those who do it professionally – but I do try always to incorporate passages, readings from the text, and when I do it, try to do it *con amore*."

He also insists that students read Shakespeare out loud. " I just point to a student and say, 'Would you mind reading Hermione's passage? Would you mind reading Theseus's speech?' It does tend to be the case that women read women's roles, but I've done cross-gendered things. The main problem with a group of inexperienced students who are not coming from their own experience as people involved on stage is to get them over the embarrassment of moving from themselves reading to themselves acting."

Cadden performs himself, reading with gusto, and participating in stagings of *Twelfth Night*. He is the most conscious of the three of the performative elements and obligations of teaching. "You are in a role," he explains, "as are the students. You can't ignore the responsibility of the role. You are expected to have knowledge, authority, and passion, and you need to fulfill those expectations. They are expected to come in with a love of learning. Alas, we are usually better at our roles than they are at theirs. But the audience is never neutral, and the classroom is a theater of mixed means." He prefers using trained actors, audio or video tapes, and theater trips to having students read. "Film clips give students freedom to see the range of representation in a scene. It's even better with actors doing the same scene different ways, as we can at the Bread Loaf Summer School where there is a resident acting ensemble. The tension then is not between actor and role, but between role and role."

Cadden also tries to exploit the possibilities of post-modern teaching, in which students are made aware of being in a dramatic space themselves. In a course on modern drama which began with Ibsen and ended with Caryl Churchill, he used the teaching staff of the course, and the teachers' different ethnic origins and sexual orientations, to illustrate the theatrical shift from fixed to fluid identities over a century.

In our Princeton seminar, teaching assistants were regularly impressed with how well performance techniques worked with all kinds of plays: "I selected the Corvino/Celia scenes from *Volpone*," wrote one, "and focused on performance and close reading of those segments. We had a few hams, who helped to wake up the others. Some of them became genuinely intrigued about the play and promises flowed that all would continue to read with interest and attention (hmm – they're beginning to tell me what I want to hear – now I know I'm turning into my mother)." When I taught Wilde's *The Importance of Being Earnest*, all the preceptors tried switching gender roles as a way to show students how stylized the dialogue is. "We read the first scene between Algy and Cecily," a preceptor reported. "Then I said, 'Okay, now switch sexes.' I thought it would be good to stick with the same people. They were a total riot! We got talking about how conversation *is* sex in Wilde." In teaching *A Doll House*, we had students reading the final few pages aloud and then asked whether "Nora can consent to a marriage contract if she isn't 'fully grown.'" We read the last scenes of *Hedda* and *Julie*, and compared suicides – "My group," said another TA, "felt that Hedda had more fun in her dying."

The performative approach, which emphasizes the dialog in a play, does not, of course, preclude or exclude other ways of teaching at the same time. Many teachers of drama actually prefer to emphasize the reading of plays, which gives value to every detail of the text. Ann Thompson, of King's College London, is among those who have critiqued the consensus that "the 'right way' to teach Shakespeare was through performance and classroom workshops," and noted the "almost total absence of literary theory and cultural politics."[17] Graham Aitken, who teaches at Chester College in England, argues that "a particular reader will always have an advantage over any theatre in the world no matter what the resources of that theatre," because reading offers more imaginative freedom. Aiken emphasizes the importance of analyzing the side-text or secondary text of the play, especially stage directions, titles, and character names. He also stresses the problems of helping student readers appreciate the non-verbal elements in a play, such as the knocking at the gate in *Macbeth*.[18] In my own teaching of Chekhov, for example, I have asked students to imagine stagings for the sound of the breaking lyre-string in *The Cherry Orchard*, as well as to explain its dramatic impact and emotional or thematic significance.

Teaching by performance has its own clichés. Everyone will recognize the hammy Shakespearean who ends every semester ("in hope of applause," Robert Watson says cynically) by intoning Prospero's speech: "Our revels now have ended."[19] Yet the self-reflexive elements of turning the play into a comment on the course can also be witty and provocative. When we read *Waiting for Godot*, a student in my Modern Drama class at Princeton wrote as his weekly required posting on the class electronic bulletin board, "They do not post."

Of course, the drama classroom is not the only academic space that reflects the subject matter. Nor is teaching and the art of performance limited to the subject of drama. As I've mentioned in chapter 2, Jyl Lynn Felman of Brandeis has written an electrifying book about pedagogy and performing, which recommends techniques of acting and improvisation to all class-room teachers.[20] Michael Conlon (Binghamton) cites psychologist Howard Gardner on the role of "performances in understanding," the use of performance to transform, reconfigure, interpret, and apply principles or data. In his own course on "Literature and Performance in Eighteenth-Century England," Conlon has students give presentations of group research projects, which have included "reconstructions of performances that took place" at weddings, masquerades, and funerals, "recreations of eighteenth-century games including a performance of the card game Ombre according to the directions in Pope's *Rape of the Lock*; a presentation on the spectacle of executions; and an eighteenth-century puppet show."[21]

In a survey course at Princeton, a TA wrote, "five women did a skit acting out Book I of *Paradise Lost*. This was quite a surprise and raised the energy of our lagging discussion very well. It was a very funny mix of Milton's lines and college-student speak: 'Beezlebub, I didn't recognize you. We are so totally fallen.' The skit did a nice job of covering what I wanted to talk about in class, and I hope the other students got more than just entertainment value from it." In her course on "Women at the Margins," Isobel Armstrong always ends by having students in groups dramatically present sections of the novels or poems to the class, and considers this exercise the most powerful moment of the course. In short, of all teaching techniques, performance can be the most active and student-centered, and can lead to engaged intellectual discovery of the text.

Chapter 6

Teaching Fiction

As teachers of literature in the twenty-first century, we are most likely to be teaching the novel. "A hundred years ago," writes W. B. Carnochan, "English departments might list perhaps one course in the novel, but poetry and drama – including Shakespeare, who still occupies the throne room of English literary studies – counted most. At mid-century, under the influence of New Criticism, poetry kept its preeminence. But after World War II, as literary criticism took a sociological turn, the novel gathered strength at the expense of poetry and drama."[1] Another genre that has gained in popularity in the literature curriculum is the short story. Especially in the United States, where the short story has claims to be an American genre, teaching short fiction offers an excellent opportunity to introduce students to the complex interactions of region, race, gender, class, and narrative technique.

So how should we teach prose fiction? Unlike poetry, drama, and even literary theory, teaching the novel has no specific, time-honored, or new trendy methodologies. Some teachers begin with the author's biography, or the historical background; I usually begin with the skin of the novel, as if it were a fruit, starting with the cover, the title, and the epigraphs, and then move to the internal structure of books, sections, chapters, and so on. Others plunge immediately into style or character, and many head straight for ideology without pausing to pass "Go."

Moreover, novels may be taught in a wide variety of contexts. In a survey course, there may be only one novel; in a seminar, all the novels of Jane Austen. Some of us will be teaching courses on the novel as a genre, others on the novel within a particular period; still others on novels by a particular kind of author. Some teachers of literature who are also novelists and short-story writers have proposed an emphasis on the parallels between the trajectories of fiction and the trajectories of an individual life. The novelist Norman Maclean, who taught at the University of Chicago, argued that fiction was a mirror of the life cycle, and that in studying it, students would see their own lives take narrative shape and meaning: "Your lives, like the stories we read and write here, will have all those elements of complication, peripeteia, resolution, etc., and it is by reading through to the end that you see the patterns and the point of it all."[2] On the other hand, Carolyn Heilbrun, who taught at Columbia and writes academic mystery novels under the name "Amanda Cross," believes that the best training for teaching fiction is writing it, and that the process of writing a novel would help a teacher understand the significance of the craft and the market: "It has often occurred to me that all teachers of literature ought to have written and published a work of fiction in order to understand something fundamental about what they teach."[3]

But not all of us have the talent, inclination, and discipline to write fiction, although we may daydream about it. Fortunately, Alex Zwerdling points out, the novel's biggest advantage for teachers is that it is much "more accessible than poetry or drama." Jerome McGann (Virginia) concurs; "so long as the fictions were not self-consciously reflexive and experimental, the undergraduates met the texts with pleasure and a certain kind of understanding."[4] Jeff Nunokawa (Princeton) emphasizes the advantage of teaching the Victorian novel: "Students love stories, and these texts are about the stories which are like those of our mass culture. I allow them to love the books, and I try to illuminate the details through cultural contextualization. I want to show them how confusing, deep and interesting details they might dismiss as sentimental can be." Americanists who teach *Adventures of Huckleberry Finn* ("the literary work most frequently taught in US colleges and high schools") say that it "always works well," citing its "thematic potency," humor, and modernity; students "find Twain refreshingly readable and full of positive energy."[5] Because they find the narrative familiar, and because they identify with the characters, students respond more readily to fiction than to other genres.

But that's also a problem. As McGann goes on to say, "that pleasure and understanding . . . proved a serious obstacle to the students' ability to think critically about the works and their own thinking." Fiction, he suggests, "draws the reader away from its medium," and "only trained readers have the skills to negotiate, back and forth, the relation between the textualities of fiction and its sublime imaginary constructs." Students who are not so trained tend to talk about characters as if they were real, and to simplify and reduce plot to events.

In order to confront and improve these critical reading skills, McGann and some of his colleagues designed a course on "Reading Fiction," linked with a seminar for graduate students on "Teaching Fiction." He has written engagingly and candidly about this experiment, with all of its surprises. Initially, McGann thought he knew exactly how he would teach the course: "We would begin with a tight and 'classic' text, *The Bride of Lammermoor*, [which] would introduce us to basic formal issues . . . From that point, we could move through a series of works that introduced the moment of modernism, and thence, to some examples of postmodern divergencies." In addition to ten fictional works from Scott to Calvino, and a course packet of criticism and theory from Forster to Bakhtin, McGann assigned a daily journal of reader response, and a research paper. "And voilà! A schematic run through two hundred years of fiction plus a serious introduction to the most up-to-date scholarship on that material."

Five weeks into the semester, they were still on *The Bride of Lammermoor*. The research paper had to go. What went wrong? McGann had asked students to prepare a recitation – a brief passage from the novel – and to explain why they found it interesting. Lo and behold, they were awkward readers, who "mangle the language when they recite." And they were very superficial explainers. So McGann slowed down, and set out to teach them how to read in detail. By the end of the semester, the students had made considerable strides as critical readers, and had notebook entries that reflected on the stages of their development. But they had read very few novels.

In other words, words McGann himself doesn't use, the students had learned to become close readers of prose fiction, and McGann had inadvertently turned a genre survey course into one of teaching from the microcosm; Sir Walter Scott became the paradigmatic novelist.[6] This experiment is a wonderful example of innovative teaching, but an expensive one. Is close reading best taught with an entire novel? And is the novel best taught through close reading? What about plot, character, structure, literary history and tradition? The novel seems to present teachers with especially difficult decisions and priorities. How can what Lawrence called "the great book of life" be squeezed into the space of a semester?

Length

Obviously, a major structural obstacle facing the teacher of the novel is its length. In his course on the Enlightenment novel, Peter V. Conroy (University of Illinois, Chicago) has to struggle to get students through the discouraging early weeks when they must read *Pamela* and *Tom Jones*.

"*Pamela*," he admits, "was the least appreciated novel on the syllabus; students suggested that it somehow be made shorter."[7] In a ten-week course on classic American literature, Steven Axelrod (University of California, Riverside) assigns two weeks for *Moby-Dick*. Still, "students generally regard *Moby-Dick* as too heavy, slow, and dense. One class memorably hissed me when I announced on the first day that they would have to read the whole book . . . I allow the students to express their legitimate reluctance to read such a difficult and intimidating book. When I keep the lines of communication open between the class members and me, their attitudes usually undergo a transformation."[8]

Alex Zwerdling, a modernist, thinks that the difficulty of assigning long books has become more acute as students have off-campus jobs, take three other courses, commute to classes, or have other personal distractions. He tries to choose shorter novels, and to break up reading assignments; but then students have problems understanding the shape of the whole text. Jeff Nunokawa struggles with "the sheer length of Victorian novels, and the practical problem of giving lectures on a long book when I can't assume they have read it all." He assigns students a certain number of pages by a given date, rather than simply assigning the novel; gives a midterm reading-check, calls on people during lectures with questions about the text, and is "emphatic about lecture attendance." The recent shift of academic interest in the Victorian period to literature of the *fin de siècle* may have something to do with the fact that the fiction of the 1880s and 1890s – Stevenson, Kipling, Haggard, Wilde, Conrad, Stoker – is simply shorter. It is much easier to plan and design a course on novels of the *fin de siècle* than to teach what James called the "loose baggy monsters" of the mid Victorians.

Another dilemma of teaching long books is managing background, and especially literary tradition, influence, and intertextuality. Many of the novels in my Contemporary Fiction course are deliberate rewritings or reimaginings of other texts; ideally students should have read *1984* and *Lord of the Flies* before we read *A Clockwork Orange*; Gabriel Garcia Marquez's *Chronicle of a Death Foretold* before Jeffrey Eugenides' *The Virgin Suicides*; *Mrs. Dalloway* before Michael Cunningham's *The Hours*. But there isn't time for everything. When I teach Cunningham, I require *Mrs. Dalloway*, and recommend the others on the syllabus; often too I will assign classic fairy tales, available on the Web, as background for Angela Carter's *The Bloody Chamber* and Annie Proulx's *Close Range*. I'll refer to the intertextual patterns in lecture, and provide some excerpts on the course website. Some students will follow up in their papers. But finally the concepts of teaching from the microcosm, close reading the microcosm, and acceptance of the impossibility of total coverage become my mantras.

Teachers of the long novel also face the problem of suspense: whether they should reveal the ending, and make it part of their overall discussion, even when some students have not been able to finish the book in time for lecture. Nunokawa says, "I try not to reveal the ending because students are so invested in pleasure of discovery. I'm reluctant to give it away."[9] I tell students that I will be talking about the ending of the book, and that they should keep up with the reading if they do not want their pleasure to be spoiled. Usually, however, I'm able to give two lectures on a novel, and save the ending until the second one. I find that one of the great advantages of teaching the American short story is its adaptability to a course structure. Not only are the stories a manageable length, but teaching them chronologically means that students grasp much of the history of literary influence within the boundaries of the syllabus.

Course Structure

How should a course on the novel be structured? Isobel Armstrong believes that her teaching of fiction has changed structurally over the years. "I've moved from teaching individual authors to thematic courses – like *work* in the Victorian novel. Of course, individual authors are still the anchor, but students don't have the time to go deeply into any one author. If I teach a period, then the century itself is the only link, and I don't think that's enough for students. In my introductory lecture in the novel course at Southampton, I identified five characteristics of the Victorian novel: affiliation, imperialism/colonialism, work, space, and gender. I think originally I made it over-complicated, but these issues could then be traced through every novel, and could be opened up as themes for a seminar."

Teaching the eighteenth-century novel, Peter Conroy establishes a routine, asking the same questions of each work. "I always begin with hints, questions, and information about structure and point of view. As we asked the same questions of different texts, we accumulated a growing set of answers that permitted comparisons and further investigations."[10] Teaching the nineteenth-century novel, Jeff Nunokawa uses paradigms of commodity capitalism, but he also reads passages aloud, and stresses close reading. "My teaching agenda is always affected by what I'm thinking at the time," he says. He refers to a wide range of movies, popular songs and television shows, but "I never use video – just quote it."

Alex Zwerdling teaches the twentieth-century novel, assigning two books by each author and compiling a course reader that allows contextual understanding with conflicting reviews, letters, and diary entries. He begins with

Portrait of the Artist as a Young Man, and in the opening classes does not provide biographical background, but plunges right into the beginning of the novel, asking students, "What here doesn't make sense to you? What do you think of the title?" Zwerdling says that "close reading is my introduction, and readerly competence the goal." But he also expects that the students will cover the canonical texts of modernist fiction.

Americanists who teach *Moby-Dick* confront some of the same problems of length, intertextuality, difficulty, and bulk of interpretation. Indeed, as Harry Levin jokes, the critical "investigation of *Moby-Dick* might almost be said to have taken the place of whaling among the industries of New England." Sanford Marovitz (Kent State University) explains that one method that "does *not* work well is dividing the novel into equal sections and assigning them on a strictly quantitative basis. Fortunately, *Moby-Dick* contains natural breaking points, cohesive and organic as it is; working according to them, the instructor can divide the book to accommodate almost any number of class periods." He uses *Moby-Dick* as the nucleus of a course of thematically-related texts from *The Odyssey* to Melville.[11]

William H. Shurr (University of Tennessee) focuses on Ahab as a tragic figure and Ishmael as a comic figure. "I assume in presenting this reading, that the student is approaching *Moby-Dick* for the first time. If the presentation seems overly structured, it is because the beginning student needs some sense of success or accomplishment in comprehending this complex masterpiece . . . The reading outlined above offers a certain aesthetic satisfaction, a sense of the whole that provides the student with some control over a major work of art, and a sense that there are still further dimensions to investigate."[12]

In sum, everyone who teaches the novel has to reach some compromise between breadth and depth, between history and intensity.

Active Learning and the Novel

Teachers of fiction have also been ingenious in finding ways to dramatize and make concrete various fictional themes. Lisa Berglund (Connecticut College) has students studying the eighteenth-century novel read for ten minutes by candlelight (preferably from an eighteenth-century edition), and then write by candlelight for ten minutes. Then the class discusses what they learned from the experiment.[13] Victorianist Crystal Downing arranges the desks to "form a unicursal labyrinth so that as students entered the room they had to zigzag to find an empty seat . . . After the laughter and groans died down, I showed a picture of an ancient unicursal labyrinth. Students slowly started talking about the labyrinth motif in *Middlemarch*."[14] William Gleason teaches a course on the American best-seller, and argues that since "best-sellers are about reading, we need to look at the moments when acts of reading are staged."

In discussion of contemporary fiction, we have asked students to name the items each member of the family in Nadine Gordimer's *July's People* takes with them when they flee Johannesburg, putting the lists on the blackboard, and then inviting the class to comment on the themes that emerge from these details. For Margaret Atwood's *The Handmaid's Tale*, Judith Jackson-Fossett (USC) came up with the idea of asking "What are the role options in Gilead and if you had to choose, which would you be?"

The Narrator and the Teacher

In general, however, the most self-reflective aspect of teaching fiction is the function of the narrator. As Robert Alter writes, "an essential defining feature of the novel is the variety, the subtlety, the unpredictability, and the quick-silver mobility of its uses of perspective."[15] We are not only the authors but also the classroom narrators of our courses. Just as teaching drama is reinforced by the theatrical space of the classroom, and teaching poetry is enabled by the oral and communal aspects of recitation, so too teaching fiction provides an opportunity to play with the teacher's narrative role and perspective. Of course, we may not be omniscient, but we can foreground and defamiliarize our reliability. In addition, some teachers may wish delib-erately to undermine or relinquish some of the authority of narrative in the classroom; we may sometimes wish to be unreliable, or self-reflexive, in order to make a point or a space for students. The ways we negotiate academic narrative can bridge the gap between experience and fiction, and serve as examples and illustrations for students of the ways narrative works, and the unconscious assumptions we make about it as readers.

Alex Zwerdling sees the narrator as an asset to students; "the narrator helps, as an explainer, introducer, facilitator, and stand-in for the reader." While Zwerdling himself has always tried to be a reliable narrator-teacher, now he feels "bored with conventional pedagogical narration; it answers too many questions with supposed finality." He now prefers to argue deliber-ately against himself, to raise questions but not to answer them.

A more dramatic demonstration of narrative is described by Brad Haseman. In his lecture on postmodernism, "four other teaching staff joined in. The session began traditionally with a lecturer dressed in a suit discussing the importance of the Enlightenment. Gradually, from the auditorium, this discourse was disrupted as the others created a landscape of contesting voices, who, from their multiple speaking positions, were able to subvert the authority of the all-knowing academic presenting from the privileged altar of knowledge . . . By the end of the event, these voices from the margins had . . . (quite literally as the suit ended scattered around the auditorium) stripped away the male position."[16] The language here conceals what really happened in the class; was it only the male position or the male lecturer who was stripped? But this piece of pedagogical guerilla theatre nonetheless offers some ideas of how the teacher's narrative role could be subverted.

Ben Knights (Durham) has written about the teacher and narrator in his study of the psychology of small discussion groups, in which he compares the teacher's role to that of the "narrator in realist fiction." In the group's collective fantasy, the teacher is assumed to have the correct answers and the authoritative interpretations, to speak for the author and to share the author's omniscience. Therefore, Knights points out, when the teacher refuses to take on this comforting role, and insists that students reach their own conclusions or accept their own uncertainties, the group's frustration can be compared to the reader's frustration with "the shift from the coherent universe and caring narrator of the 'readable' nineteenth-century novel to the ambiguous and unreliable narrator of the twentieth-century one."[17]

In a course on fiction, narrative, or the novel, these implicitly psychological parallels become available for our most imaginative, explicit, intellectual deployment. Every literary technique of realist, modernist, or postmodernist/metafictional narrative can be adapted into a pedagogical technique as well; every literary convention of narrative structure can be turned into a classroom practice.

In my own teaching of the novel and the short story, I have long experimented with ways to use pedagogy itself as a mirror or laboratory of narrative. That effort requires the teacher's triple attention to levels of information and understanding. Students first need to analyze the technique in the text; second, to have it named and defined through handouts, or course webpage sites, so that they can identify and recognize it; and third, to see how it operates in the classroom, and to imagine for themselves alternative ways to represent it. In working with the Victorian novel, for example, the teacher can foreground conventions of realist narrative in the texts, and also demonstrate their conventionality by incorporating some of the same devices into the syllabus – the three-part structure, the double ending, the direct address to the reader/student. In teaching fiction of the *fin de siècle*, I have tried to construct the course as a frame narrative, in imitation of the technique of Kipling, Stevenson, James, Wells, and Conrad. In my own teaching, I am asking the students the question posed by late nineteenth-century narrative experiment: why is *this* person telling us *this* story?

Film and video clips offer the students opportunities to compare the ways that narrators and narrative techniques may be represented in another medium. Voice-over, montage, flashbacks, color, sound, have to stand in for the narrator. How are unreliable narrators handled in film? How are levels of consciousness conveyed?

In teaching postmodern novels, I organize the texts thematically, as well as chronologically, in terms of dystopias, female gothics, fairy tales, re-imaginings, magical realism, postcolonialism, metafictions; and theoretically, in terms of defamiliarization, intertextuality, breaking the frame, hybridity, and hyperreality. All of these can be made part of the technique of the course as well, incorporated into lectures, and made available for student discussion. Moreover, the structures, packages, and conventions of higher education can be used to remind students of the marketing of fiction; the teacher, like the author in any period, has to contend with the business that controls access to a public.

Teaching a Course on the Novel

Defining the overall themes and learning objectives of a fiction course, and fitting them into the temporal grid of the term, can be a real challenge. In my Contemporary Fiction course, I came up with the following:

> Contemporary fiction has no literary canon, and a relatively small critical archive, so we need to come to it equipped with the reading techniques and intellectual resources that enable us to make our own judgments and enhance our own understanding and enjoyment. I have designed this course to introduce you to some of the genres, modes, and techniques of contemporary fiction, including dystopia, fairy tale, fabulism, magical realism, postcolonialism, and metafiction.
>
> Contemporary fiction is also the product of an industry undergoing drastic and unpredictable change. As we enter the twenty-first century, the publishing, the marketing and even the reading of fiction have been so transformed that some pessimists predict the death of literature and reading, while others, including myself, see unprecedented opportunities. How will the internet, electronic publishing, Oprah's Book Club, Amazon.com, cyberspace reading clubs, bookstore coffee shops, celebrity author book tours, and other contemporary phenomena affect the way we read and write fiction in the future? Will traditional assumptions about

nationality, race, ethnicity, age, and gender continue to segment the literary market, or will books like the Harry Potter series confound it? What are the literary effects of movies and television, and how will new media change fiction?

Addressing these questions will require active and interactive involvement on our part, and I expect participants in this course to be players rather than passive listeners and spectators. That means keeping up with the reading and coming to both large and small classes (i.e. lectures and precepts) ready to engage with texts and ideas. Each of you will be required to post comments and responses to your reading every week on the electronic discussion page for your precept. These postings will be the starting-point for precept discussions.

By the end of this course, you should be able to identify and evaluate the techniques contemporary writers use in their fiction; to locate new works within a historical context and aesthetic tradition; to do close readings of passages from a novel and show their relation to the whole; to analyze (and even imitate) a writer's style; to compare novels and their adaptations for other media in terms of the narrative conventions of each medium; to form and defend critical judgments about new writing; and to analyze the relationship between the business of publishing and the development of fiction in a contemporary context.

Beginnings

In my fiction classes, I try to incorporate elements of narrative into the teaching process, and also make students aware of how these elements operate to define experience as story. I compare lecturing to narration in the novel, demonstrate ways to vary and violate it, and encourage students to think of how it might be done. (Once, to show how you could rupture or break the narrative frame of the classroom, I had a graduate student interrupt the lecture by loudly announcing he had a pizza to deliver to a student. Readers will recognize the homage to *Fast Times at Ridgmont High*. But every semester provides its own spontaneous frame-breakers, from a squirrel running around the auditorium to fire drills to students streaking.)

I also emphasize narrative conventions of temporality – beginning, middle, and end. A semester has its beginning, the first class, the first discussion; its middle, usually punctuated by an exam, a break, or a paper; and its end, or last lecture and final exam. These moments of introduction, continuity, complication, and closure have obvious similarities to the rhythms of stories or novels.

In my contemporary fiction class, I structure the syllabus and the course itself around these temporal and spatial elements in the novel, and in our semester. The first class is titled "Beginnings." I believe that the beginning of a course, or a lecture, or a discussion, is its most important moment. I ask the students when they think the "contemporary" begins. Is it coterminous with my life span? With that of the students? (A rapidly widening gap.) Is the contemporary limited to living writers? Is it about a subject matter, or a style? Did it begin in 1963, along with sexual intercourse, the end of the Chatterley ban, and the Beatles' first LP?

Then we talk, with the aid of a handout and the first paragraphs of *Neuromancer*, *Trainspotting*, and *Push*, about how contemporary novels begin. Beginnings are important in twentieth-century fiction, especially American fiction, which can't hang around to work out all the genealogical and historical details but has to grab the reader's attention right away. As Daniel Menaker, the former fiction editor of the *New Yorker*, says about the first sentence of a story, "when you meet someone, what is the first sentence that they say to you that makes you want to keep listening?"[18]

Finally, I also use film and video clips to illustrate cinematic conventions of beginnings, from Disney cartoons to realism to the avant-garde.

Middles

Middles of courses involve assignments, and they are different for each group of novels. For the contemporary fiction course, I give students a handout on close reading, ask them to practice it in their precepts, and to write a one-page close reading of a paragraph from one of the novels. Here are my instructions:

> Close reading is slow reading, a deliberate attempt to detach ourselves from the magical power of story-telling and pay attention to language, imagery, allusion, intertextuality, syntax, and form. It is one of the major techniques of contemporary literary criticism. In a sense, close reading is a form of defamiliarization we use in order to break through our habitual and casual reading practices. It forces us to be active rather than passive consumers of the text. Since novels are very long texts, we don't attempt a close reading of the whole book. Instead, we look at particular important sentences, sometimes even phrases; we may group them together to reach an interpretation or to illustrate an observation.
>
> To learn how to do close reading, start by selecting a paragraph and look at it sentence by sentence. Why does the author use particular words,

images, grammatical constructions, even punctuation? How do these choices affect your responses as a reader? What other choices might the author have made? Are there allusions or quotations from other works? How does the verbal texture of this paragraph illuminate the theme of the book?

Practicing the technique in precept, a TA commented "We took the phrase 'I sit in my chair' [in *The Handmaid's Tale*] and analyzed it word by word. We did not consume too much class-time doing this exercise but I think most everyone found the experience empowering . . . The single English major argued that to close read, or, in his words, 'micro-manage' a syllable/word/phrase/passage is to sap it of its vitality. I guess that the others were so delighted with seeing the possibilities of close-reading that, unprompted by me, a lively, coherent, useful debate emerged about the efficacy and ethics of the practice." In another precept, the TA offered "three passages from Martha Stewart for close reading – an exercise designed to get to questions of what constitutes an ideal domesticity, without imposing any fears that there was a correct interpretation they were guessing at. The fifteen minutes we spent on Stewart and the fifteen minutes we spent tying it to *Little Women* were perhaps the most fun and informative I have yet shared with a class." The written close readings are not graded, but we comment on them in detail, and discuss the results with precepts.

Another technique I use with my classes is what I call the "conversion experience" – to take a passage from a novel with a strong style, and translate it into another idiom; or to apply a technique of a story or novel to another experience. I've had excellent results from students rendering the Nadsat of Alex in Anthony Burgess's *A Clockwork Orange* into other kinds of slang, or making up to-do lists in the style of Lorrie Moore in *Self-Help*. Students enjoy doing these exercises, and often do them a lot better than I could; in addition, the assignment makes them concentrate on style and detail. Here are some examples:

1 Burgess in Princeton-speak, circa 1995: "The day was very different from the night. Me and my buds and all the rest of the slackers owned the night, and the meddling class sat stagnating in their condos while those hipsters Connie and Dan sat on their retinas, but the day was for profs and 'rents and there always seemed to be more proctors or narcs about during the day too."

2 Burgess in New Mexico cowboy-speak, circa 1999: "The four of us were dressed alike in the style of the time, which was always a pair of tight wrangler boot-cuts, along with the good old gut-protector, as we

referred to it after many a saloon brawl, glamorizing the strap of useless leather we claimed we needs to keep our pants up. Each of us had a different one of these gut protectors, symbolizing sumtin from our lives; I got one with a bear on it, Clint had a six-shooter on his, Dan had one with the horse kickers on 'em, and poor dum John had a bale of hay on his. John never having had a clue about the ways of the men, had about the IQ of a mule, definitely the most injun of us."

I am constantly looking for assignments that do not require students to write essays – group presentations, annotated bibliographies, anthologies – whatever allows bright students who do not write as well as they think to show what they understand. In literary study, too often all assignments depend on writing skills. One of my perpetual dilemmas in teaching literature is the convention of the paper assignment – two short and one long, or two medium and a final examination, spread out throughout the semester like a patient etherized upon a table. At Princeton, students expect a lot of guidance about paper topics and process, although they also like to have some choice. Elsewhere, notably in Britain, undergraduates are expected to produce a lengthy research essay in every course. My problem is always how to make these papers more sequential and cumulative, and more focused, more than simply paper A, and then paper B.

Sometimes I have had students select from a list of themes, and look at the same theme or problem in two papers on different sets of texts, with the final examination devoted to an overview of what studying the evolution of this theme has taught them. That has not always worked well, because students must make a choice before they have had time to read the stories or novels, and many would prefer to write about whatever interests them most, rather than following an assigned topic. Nevertheless, even those students who complained said that the focus had sharpened their critical writing.

The assignment worked best in a freshman honors seminar on Scott Fitzgerald, whose papers are all at Princeton's Firestone Library. Students selected a theme at the beginning of the term from a list I had prepared, and concentrated their writing on that throughout. In their first paper, they examined it in Fitzgerald's work through the 1920s; in the second paper they looked at his work in the 1930s; and in their final paper, they revised and combined the two, using historical background material, criticism, and biography to deepen and enrich their analysis. In their conclusion, I asked them to address questions of judgment and evaluation. "How fully did FSF come to grips with the theme in the course of his career? How important is it to his writing as a whole? In which works does he handle it most effectively and why? Is there a chronology to his treatment and how can you account for it?"

Endings

The final class is titled "Endings." Ending in narrative is always poignant. Even the ending of the narrative of a course has its melancholy edge, although the students may be eagerly rushing to catch planes back home for the holidays and you may be just as eager to see the back of them for a few weeks. Perhaps it is always ourselves we mourn for in the end of any season, although the autumn one usually feels sadder than the spring/summer one, with its metaphors of commencement and renewal. For teachers, every ending of a semester is a signal of time passing, the students staying eternally young while we ourselves grow older. But for students too there is some sense of separation and regret, as they close their notebooks. Especially in the fall, I try to end the course with one of the more life-affirming books of our age, as a sort of Christmas present. In the last discussion groups, there are other needs to be met that are more intellectual. Howard Keeley, one of my most gifted teaching assistants, would stagger in to the last discussion meeting carrying all the texts of the course, to show the students what they had done, how far they had come.

I use the final lecture of the course to reflect on the ambiguous, open endings of many contemporary novels. I talk about the conventions of closure, the ending tagmemes, of fiction and story. In the classic novel, critics argue, the endings bear the moral freight of the entire book. We look at the last lines and last words of the novels we have read, with the help of a handout I have prepared, and discuss contemporary embarrassment about endings, the postmodern evasion of the grand climax, and the trend towards the anti-climactic. Postmodern novels do not always end, but stop.

I relate this phenomenon in the lecture to my own embarrassment about endings, my feeling that a big wind-up is hammy and corny, and should be avoided, while I make a dignified withdrawal. Since at Princeton students traditionally applaud the last lecture of a course, there is the additional tension of all of us knowing that I will have to make a graceful or rushed exit, my wish not to milk the applause by leaving slowly, and my awareness that my colleagues in the building have an inbuilt applause meter by which they are measuring the volume and duration of each other's end-of-term bows. Also at our backs we hear the winged chariots of student evaluations hurrying near, which can never be ecstatic enough for the poor professorial ego. These are the academic equivalents of Jane Austen's observations at the end of *Northanger Abbey* that we can all see by the dwindling number of pages that the denouement is nigh.

But I can also deflect some of the anxiety by ending with a discussion of the end or death of the novel, always predicted, yet so far deferred, and with my conviction that if they keep reading, and buying, fiction, the novel will live on. The afterlife of teaching fiction is the conviction that our courses too are open-ended, cyclical, and that they will begin again, not only with our next semester, but also within the minds of the students who have become devoted readers.

Chapter 7
Teaching Theory

The Posttheory Generation in the Classroom

Sandra Gilbert tells a story about serving on a search committee at Princeton in the 1980s that interviewed a candidate whose dream course would be " 'theory and – and, um – ' (there was a long silence) 'theory and *non*theory.' Our chair asked, '*non*theory, what's that?' And she said 'well, nontheory, like, *you* know, poems, stories, plays.' "[1] The anecdote illustrates the difference between two academic generations. Gilbert's (and my own) generation made our careers during an era when we and others around us were theorizing because we were dealing with new bodies of literature, by women or black or postcolonial writers, about whom we had urgent new questions. Looking back at this period in the second edition of *Literary Theory*, Terry Eagleton reflects that "the 1970s, or at least the first half of them, were a decade of social hope, political militancy, and high theory. This conjuncture was not accidental; theory of a grand kind tends to break out when routine social or intellectual practices have come unstuck, run into trouble, and urgently need to rethink themselves." With hitherto marginalized or excluded groups entering the universities as students and teachers, Eagleton adds, "it was no longer possible to take for granted what literature was, how to read it, or what social functions it might serve."[2] As the 1970s progressed, theory was the ticket to intellectual and academic legitimacy; inventing a new terminology, coming up with general principles and recurrent themes, hypothesizing ways of reading, elaborating on the relationship between dominant and minority literary traditions, offered a strategy for canonical revision and change. But above all, theory came out of specific literary questions for which we wanted answers.

103

The work of the grand masters of European theory, including Barthes, Althusser, Lacan, de Man, and Foucault, was very different, and brought linguistic, philosophical, psychoanalytic, and political questions to bear on fundamental issues of meaning, representation, mythology, and desire. All of these men had died by 1984, and, despite the status of other philosophical theorists including Derrida, Kristeva, and Habermas, in the preface to the paperback edition of *The Pleasures of Reading in an Ideological Age*, another critic looking backward, Robert Alter, recalls that when he wrote the book in the late 1980s, "the prestige of 'grand theory' in American literary studies, though immense, was just beginning to wane."[3]

To Alter, this decline was basically a good thing. But with the waning of grand theory came more theory, a parallel generation of applied theorists, including such Americans as Frederick Jameson, Stephen Greenblatt, Stanley Fish, Eve Kosofsky Sedgwick, and Judith Butler, whose work became the subject as well as the adjunct of literature courses for graduate students, and then for undergraduates as well. For young graduate students and professors, theory was no longer something they did, but rather something they studied. Jeffrey Williams calls this cohort, which came into the profession in the late 1980s and the 1990s, the "posttheory generation."[4] Their orientation to literary theory is more academic than active, but also, as Gilbert's story suggests, they see theory as a genre among others.

The institutionalization of courses in literary theory around the late 1980s did not immediately bring along changes in pedagogical methods. Martin Bickman reports that during a series of MLA interviews in the early 1990s, he "asked the candidates, most of whom were still in graduate school, if their theoretically more advanced teachers ran their classrooms any differently from their more traditional ones. [But] . . . the structures of authority in the classroom itself, the ways in which students and teachers interacted – or didn't interact – remained untouched. Despite poststructuralist skepticism about the validity of any single interpretation, despite insights about the transactional, emotive, and subjective aspects of the reading process, teachers of graduate students more often than not droned on themselves – often about these very ideas – without enacting any of these notions in the classroom."[5]

Graduate seminars are the most traditionally structured and pedagogically resistant to change of all literature courses. Still, reviewing the teaching of literary theory at all levels in 1994, D. G. Myers sees three dominant and unsatisfactory modes. First, the "taxonomical survey," in which "what is imparted in the classroom are the propositional contents of various and differing bodies of doctrine." Second, the heuristic concept of theory as a set of practical tools and techniques, with "different theories abridged and combined into a strategy for the interpretation of texts." Myers sees both of these approaches as part of a "pedagogical regime of authoritarianism," in which the "very structure of the transaction between teacher and student is one of supervision and correction, entailing authority and deference." Third, the radical approach, attempting to "empower students by showing them how to disclose the ideological assumptions behind any cultural perform-ance, and then to re-politicize their newfound knowledge by placing it in the context of the class struggle." This oppositional pedagogy, Myers argues, is deeply flawed as well, partly because of the ironies of the privileged aca-demic elite confronting political power in such a hypocritical, "weirdly timid" and second-hand way, and partly because its very didacticism contradicts the openness and questioning that theory stands for.

In principle, Myers argues, theory should be the most problem-based and problematized part of the literary curriculum. "I believe," he writes, "that the only way to teach literary theory is to take issue with it." Something of value can be retrieved from each of the three standard approaches: "the taxonomical survey recognizes that literary theory is a substantial historical achievement that ought to be apportioned a share of every serious student's literary education. The heuristic method – applied theory, as it might be called – discerns that literary theory is something that must be engaged in, not passively learned about. Radical monism is a summons to remember always that the role of theory is to be oppositional." But these can be com-bined in a practice that always presumes "that the texts on one's syllabus are in error. They are to be swallowed only if, upon consideration, they succeed in making their case." Indeed, he concludes, "perhaps it is smarter to assign our antagonists . . . Surely the theorists can withstand rough handling, and if nothing else the class sessions will be lively. Although this approach may not be for everyone, it should appeal to those of us who enjoy the contention of theory."[6]

Myers's essay is the most rigorous critique of the teaching of theory, and assumes a level of intellectualism in the students, and effortless and neutral leadership in the teacher, that few undergraduate classrooms could provide; but many voices have joined him. Donald G. Marshall (University of Illinois, Chicago) explains that teaching theory as "an array of schools . . . seems commonsensical, [but] doing so distorts students' understanding of the role theory ought to play in the study of literature and indeed dis-torts their understanding of theory itself . . . They learn to look for explicit general propositions that can be extracted and articulated into a system. What students draw in this way from a single essay or excerpt they will gen-eralize still further by treating it as exemplary of a school."[7] As the film theorist D. N. Rodowick urges, "we must break down whenever possible

the consumerist approach to learning, by which the teacher is selling something that students may or may not buy. Instead, the history of theory should
be presented as an ongoing debate in which students are encouraged to participate."[8]

The open-ended problems students confront in studying literary theory
offer opportunities for literature teachers to experiment with a variety of
collaborative and innovative course structures. Since the mid-1990s, on the
undergraduate level, faculty from the second "posttheory generation" have
discussed and implemented precisely those questions of connecting theory
to student-centered classroom practice. Their innovations, supported more
recently by developments in the use of technology and computers, and bringing popular culture, cyberspace, hypertext, and interactive software to bear
on teaching, have made theory one of the most exciting and creative fields
in literary pedagogy. *Teaching Contemporary Theory to Undergraduates*,
edited by Dianne F. Sadoff and William E. Cain, is a useful guide to this new
work.

The impetus for transformation came first from feminist criticism, which
questioned the traditional teacher–student power relationship, as well as
the tacit values of competition, emotionlessness, and mastery in the "banking
model" of education, and advocated "being inductive, cooperative, attentive
to the subjective, student-centered."[9] Teachers of postmodern theory agreed
that they needed to change the New Critical model of the authoritarian
teacher giving out the week's interpretation. "The teacher as New Critic,"
Dianne Sadoff (Miami University) notes, "tended to stage his readings
as performance . . . The brilliant lecture, studded with quotations from the
text, with references to tenor and vehicle, with rhetorical paradoxes, became
the pedagogical norm . . . this pedagogical strategy . . . assumed the teacher's
authority, mastery of his material, and control of his necessarily passive
and submissive students."[10] In deliberate contrast, teachers like Susan Lanser
(Maryland) added to their theory courses "several student-centered pedagogical practices: small groups, student-led discussions, collectively created
agendas, and 'free space' – open time at the beginning of each class in which
any questions can be raised."[11]

Others raised the questions of the practical relationship between theory
and pedagogy. Diana Fuss (Princeton) asked "what contributions has theory
made to pedagogy? How has the teaching of theory changed our theories
of teaching? Is the theoretical classroom different, in any philosophical
or structural way, from other (supposedly non-theoretical) classrooms?"[12]
Martin Bickman observes that "pedagogy is the area in which we can most
clearly and immediately test our theories of reading, of making meaning,

of how language and the mind work. And it is the best source of data for constructing these theories." He suggested that "reader-response theory in particular seemed to promise strategies for unifying theory and pedagogy."

Fear of Theory

Teaching theory was once the only part of the curriculum about which professors expressed ambivalence and even terror. John Kucich admits that "when I was first assigned to teach a theory course in my department's honors program, I tried everything I could to get out of it."[13] Susan Lanser confesses that "in the fall of 1988, during the depths of the presidential campaign, my life as a teacher reached an all-time low. Never had I taught an entire course in literary theory to undergraduates, and never had I faced a class – let alone an honors class – persistently frustrated by the curriculum . . . By mid-October, the students said they felt overwhelmed, paralyzed, bogged down, and off balance – and so did I."[14]

Diana Fuss points out that "students worry that, like the latest military weapons system, the newest theory will be obsolete long before it becomes operational; according to this view, investing in theory constitutes a waste of time, an inefficient expenditure of energy and intellect."[15] And Dianne Sadoff sees part of the ritual as warning students that the going will be rough. "Like other teachers of theory," she writes, "I had cautioned my students on the first day of class that reading is not an innocent activity."[16]

Theory in Practice

But some of these fears subsided as literature teachers began to reconceive the theory course as a set of problems rather than a list of the newest and most forbidding "isms." Andy Mousley at DeMontfort University in Leicester teaches theory to undergraduates, but has moved away from "isms" to topics, such as value, the canon, gender, and interpretation. As Andrew Bennett and Nicholas Royle argue in their textbook, "theory – especially when it takes the forms of *isms* – can often be intimidating, or else, frankly, boring." Instead they present "brief essays on a range of key critical concepts," including readers and reading, the author, the uncanny, narrative, sexual difference, ideology, desire, and pleasure.[17] Some of the best "theory" courses are based on literary problems: realism, value, texts and contexts, cultures and subcultures.

More generally, teachers of literary theory have looked for ways to organize their courses around issues, questions, and tasks that students can carry out themselves.

Mark Hanson (Princeton) stresses that theory offers students "tools to think more deeply about their own lives and situations, beyond literary arcane problems." His midterm assignment is to have students analyze the university honor code, and he builds "assignments that point toward an issue." For Hanson, teaching theory means "active learning, turning the problems into action."[18]

Other teachers of theory have found ways to connect to what students know, and to overcome their resistance, with patience and imagination. Diana Fuss has discovered that "the actual practice of teaching theory to undergraduates has forced me to acknowledge the importance of what one might call leisure time in the act of theorizing, and it has taught me to adapt my teaching strategy to keep the reading load to a minimum and creating, wherever possible, 'open spaces' the students themselves can fill with suggestions for new approaches to reading the most stubborn texts."[19]

John Kucich used to assign Saussure at the beginning of the course; now he starts with the Romantics, and with the more accessible ideas of the author. He usually begins class "with a short, absolutely unoriginal outline of the basic ideas in the day's reading assignment, something just detailed enough to circumvent misunderstanding and to bolster my students' self-confidence. This preparation often encourages them to express some very acute responses during the rest of the session."[20] David Downing organizes the syllabus in terms of three "cultural revolutions," involving theories of literature, and begins by having students write "a brief institutional autobiography or narrative account of their experience of English in school and classroom settings." He tells the students to regard his syllabus as a narrative he has "authored and plotted," which they will read and study like a novel; but in the last four weeks of the course, they will write a new ending."[21]

Susan Lanser offers several recommendations about a "problem-posing" mode of teaching theory. First, she teaches multiple perspectives on each topic. More broadly, she follows a three-stage model of "description, diagnosis, and reconstruction," adapted from the pedagogy specialist Ira Schor. In the description stage, when students are encountering theoretical texts for the first time, "every idea is presented as provisional and I encourage students to see what I don't see." She keeps lecturing minimal, but provides a weekly reading guide, including questions, "ways of coping with the material," and "practical exercises . . . that allow students to test their grasp of concepts." In the diagnosis stage, students are expected to test out

the theories and evaluate them. "Instead of taking the position that a particular theory is good for the students, we ask together what the theory is
good for." At this point, students work in small groups on their own, with
the option of reporting back to the entire group. Students also write short
position papers, which they read aloud. In the final phase, students work
together to critique the course, propose an alternative syllabus, or write
essays showing the relevance of theory to other courses. In one term, Lanser
boldly had students critique drafts of her own essay on feminist criticism and
Charlotte Perkins Gilman's *The Yellow Wallpaper*. Overall, this pedagogical
model aims to give students the tools to "participate in the profession and
to engage the issues facing it."[22]

Assignments and exercises in problem-based theory courses are ingenious.
Gary Waller has students read Raymond Williams's *Key Words* and construct
their own history of a key word not in the book.[23] Lynette Felber begins by
assigning Susan Leonardi's *PMLA* essay on recipes in literature, "to shock
students and broaden their expectations about what constitutes literary
criticism."[24] Sandra Grayson has students who are silent in discussion summarize the day's debate.[25] Laurie Finke (Kenyon), one of the editors of the
new *Norton Anthology of Criticism and Theory*, begins her "lesson in the
microtheory of social constructivism by asking students to consider a campus
map and then taking a leisurely and aimless walk around the campus."[26]

Teaching a Literary Theory Course

The best place to find models and ideas for teaching theory now is the Web,
where a number of teachers, following the example of Alan Liu's monumental Voice of the Shuttle, are building sites and posting their syllabi,
assignments, exams, and synopses of classes. An ideal and inspiring example
is that of Professor Dino Franco Felluga, at Purdue. Felluga typifies the
posttheory generation; a Canadian who did his undergraduate work at the
University of Western Ontario, he completed his PhD on the verse novel at
Santa Barbara with Alan Liu and Garrett Stewart, and then did a post-doc at
Stanford with Barbara Gelpi and Regenia Gagnier. His website offers the
syllabi for several of his undergraduate and graduate courses, on subjects from
nineteenth-century fiction to trauma theory; and an undergraduate guide to
criticism and theory that students can study on their own. All of his courses
incorporate a significant amount of theory, and all are student-centered. For
anyone of my generation still wondering about how to teach theory and nontheory; or for those in the posttheory generation seeking inspiration, Felluga's
website, http://icdweb.cc.purdue.edu/~felluga, is the place to go.

In his ambitious course on "Great Narrative Works," he uses *Paradise Lost* along with *Citizen Kane*, Conrad and *Apocalypse Now*, and theories of narratology in literature and film; but with impressively sophisticated and lively exercises for students all along, including a mock-trial of Satan in which they are the jury. Listed among his "Class Policies" is "Class Participation [class, Germanic, kla/kela: to shout, roar]: Dialogue is the only path to knowledge; here we do it verbally and I do expect you to roar, or at least speak. I believe in an interactive classroom in which we learn from each other and respect (although not necessarily agree with) the opinions of others. Remember, if you count the Trial of Satan, 20% of the grade will be given on the basis of your class participation."

Felluga illustrates what he means by the interactive classroom by writing and posting a synopsis of the class discussion for every meeting. On the very first day of class on August 22, 2000, for example, he showed the first minute of *Citizen Kane*, and had the students try to figure out from the images in this brief sequence – a "No Trespassing" sign, some gates and fences, and a mansion in the distance – what they infer. In other words, he has the students work out the difference between the very basic "story" and the much more complex "discourse" of the narrative. Felluga gives his own narrative of the discussion, identifying each student's contribution to an analysis of director Orson Welles's techniques, including gothic images of the haunted house, lighting, gloomy music, the sense of mystery and trespass, the use of house and landscape as psychological metaphor for Kane, camera angles, and literary echoes. As Felluga concludes, "Nothing is actually happening in this scene and, yet, students were able to determine all the major interpretive issues of the film from this apparently innocuous first scene, suggesting indeed that the discursive presentation of a story and not the story itself is, in fact, the heart of the narrative."[27] In subsequent classes, he has the students continue to make their own discoveries, learn the theoretical terminology, and apply their insights to increasingly complex literary texts.

Too often, the problem-based elements of a theory course consist of the students' critique of the course itself, but courses like "Great Narrative Works" are a model of the ways that theory can be used to help students work out central literary problems. Making theory relevant to students' lives is a worthy cause, but theory developed in order to answer literary questions, and the excitement of that inquiry can be recaptured in the classroom by demanding and imaginative teaching.

Chapter 8

Teaching Teachers

Opinion surveys of graduate students carried out over the past few years have all shown that students want more training in how to teach literature. Indeed, one reason that graduate students in the University of California system were unionizing was to protest at being thrown into classrooms without preparation. "It was scary," said one. "I knew the material, but I felt like I needed a lot more help." When I was starting out as a TA at the University of California at Davis, and for many years afterward at Rutgers, there was no training but there were mandatory class visitations and reports for all untenured faculty, a kind of pedagogical taxation without representation. The situation is much improved today. In the UK, the government established a national Institute for Learning and Teaching (ILT) in 1999, to which faculty apply, and which aims to license and certify academic professionalism in teaching. The English Subject Centre, one of 22 subject-specific teaching centers, and DUET (Developing University English Teaching), sponsor colloquia and conferences on teaching, and supplement induction programs for new teachers on individual campuses. Teaching is audited too, by the much-disputed Quality Assurance Agency (QAA). The success of Britain's Open University has also spurred much research and debate about distance learning and ways to train teachers to conduct it.

In the US, too, books, journals, and websites that provide detailed information about these matters are now widely available. English departments provide some training for new TAs, often in workshops led by experienced TAs. In addition, many universities now have their own centers for teaching and learning, which publish handbooks and newsletters, provide background resources, and will send a consultant to visit your classroom and even to videotape it. Sue Lonoff, who is the Associate Director of the Derek Bok

111

Center for Teaching and Learning at Harvard, argues that videotape "remains the best instrument we have for mapping the dynamic of the classroom," and that "during filming, both teachers and students quickly shed their self-consciousness." Overall, she writes persuasively, for junior faculty, taping a class discussion "may be less disruptive for teachers and students than a visit from a senior faculty member." In any case, analysis of the tape is confidential, and consultants focus on helping the instructor develop self-awareness about class dynamics and process. As one Harvard consultant says, "by the time the instructors teach here, they're very good at content; what they're less aware of is the ways in which students need the skills to deal with the content, to make their own arguments both orally and in written form."[1] Another way to get feedback on class dynamics is to have graduate students observe each other's classes, and exchange responses.

I've always believed that graduate faculty members are responsible for preparing their students to teach, and that they shouldn't relegate the task to other teaching assistants – but I can also understand why professors are reluctant to step forward. Setting ourselves up as experts on teaching feels like tempting fate. Which of us dares to volunteer our own classes as teaching laboratories? Who should be assigned to teach teaching? The director of graduate studies? The director of undergraduate studies? Someone else altogether?

Yet it shouldn't be such a problem. According to one specialist on teaching, "the resources needed for effective training of college teachers are readily available on every campus. Most academic departments have one or more professors acknowledged to be outstanding teachers by both their peers and their students. They have learned to put together lectures that are both rigorous and stimulating and homework assignments and tests that are comprehensive, challenging, instructive, and fair. They have found ways to motivate students to want to learn, to co-opt them into becoming active participants in the learning process, to help them develop critical and creative thinking and problem-solving abilities."[2] Further, teaching about teaching is dialogic; it's everyone's task, not the province of the expert. Martin Bickman adds that "helping graduate students learn to teach should not be considered just another item on our to-do list, but rather an energizing and integrating activity that can help us all put together the various parts of our professional lives."[3] Having taken the chance myself, I can say that I gained much more in intellectual excitement and new ideas than I risked in putting my ego on the line.

But teaching others how to teach also has to be more than passing on your own tips, or trying to clone yourself. It takes as much preparation as any other kind of course. Kenneth Eble urges that meeting the needs of beginning college and university teachers "must be an integral part of the program, as highly respected, as subject to the involvement of mentors, as capable of supervision and examination, and as favorable to shows on individual initiative and imagination as any other part of the program." Eble insists that "seminars in teaching should be a routine part of graduate study for all students planning to teach. They should carry credit and be as demanding as any graduate work."[4]

Moreover, the teaching seminar itself must model the approaches you want to discuss. Here, as elsewhere, learning is most effective when it is active and interactive. Ideally, graduate students will also be doing some teaching themselves as you begin to work together. Teaching can't be taught apart from practice and hands-on experience. Moreover, we need to understand how graduate students learn to be teachers. Students do not come to teaching as blank slates. They have already internalized theories of teaching based on their own experience as learners. Jody Nyquist and Jo Sprague see three developmental stages for beginning teachers: senior learners, colleagues-in-training, and junior colleagues. In these stages, they move from overriding concerns about themselves – whether they know enough, and whether they are liked and respected – to concerns about skills, and finally to concerns about student learning, and effective collaborative instruction.[5]

Beginning teachers are most concerned with content and mastery of the subject. But, as Diana Laurillard explains, "teachers need to know more than just their subject. They need to know the ways it can come to be understood, the ways it can be misunderstood, what counts as understanding; they need to know how individuals experience the subject. However, they are neither required nor enabled to know these things."[6] Teaching graduate students how to teach works best if it goes beyond one-on-one mentoring, because sharing information about the ways undergraduates react to material or a method accelerates this learning process.

In the series of teaching seminars I directed at Princeton, participants were all engaged in teaching precepts for a variety of courses in English and comparative literature. We met once a week, read essays and books on pedagogy, and looked at teaching videos from Harvard, MIT, Stanford, and Michigan. English department faculty and the director of the Teaching Center visited the seminar for discussions of such topics as course design, lecturing, grading, time management, and teaching portfolios. We read about the case-study method developed at Harvard Business School, and used some of their excellent teaching cases in *Teaching and the Case Method*, edited by Louis B. Barnes, C. Roland Christensen, and Abby J. Hansen. A particularly stimulating case is called "An Earthquake had Started." In it, a young political science instructor is leading a tutorial on when a country is justified in going to war. They first mention self-defense and national security, then moral concerns about another country, then genocide. He calls on Tracy, a very bright black student:

> "So what do you think? Was the Holocaust a just cause for war?"
> "No, I don't think that's a reason to go to war."
> "Why not?"
> "Because they weren't Christians."
> It felt like an earthquake had started. I paused.
> "What do you mean?"
> "In the first place, I'm not sure it happened the way they said it did, and in the second place I'm sure they had their reasons."
> Stunned silence.[7]

What should the instructor do? This case raised powerful questions for all of us, and foregrounded issues of multiculturalism, free speech, and pedagogical ethics. Many TAs felt strongly that holocaust denial had to be condemned immediately. Others thought it was safest to ignore the comment. Eventually we decided that the next step for the instructor was to invite the student to explain herself more fully, with the idea that before any further discussion could go on, everyone had to be clear on what had been said and intended. Discussing this case gave everyone more confidence in dealing with explosive classroom issues.

We also brainstormed ways to turn literary issues and problems into open-ended cases that could generate powerful student discussion. But we quickly discovered that cases naturally emerged from our own teaching week by week. The most useful and memorable aspect of the seminar turned out to be the electronic discussion board on which all of us posted descriptions of our various precepts for the week. We used these postings to kick off the next week's discussion. They included not only cases of students approaching literary problems, but also many real-life cases of problems that came up in classroom process. Karen Beckman (Rochester) found the idea of the electronic bulletin board "intimidating" at first, and worried that it would become a competition to "show off who has the best lesson plan." But she soon found that "people began utilizing the space of the list to ask for help and advice and this took the pressure to perform away." Sally Bachner too found that "the time involved was well repaid."

Most of our time in the Cotsen Seminar was spent discussing discussion, since graduate teaching assistants primarily lead precept meetings for large undergraduate lecture courses. All of the students struggled with the difference between the level of discussion in their graduate seminars and the level of the undergraduate courses they were teaching. All worried initially about how to convey content, information, and critical sophistication to their jaded, recalcitrant or aesthetically naive students. But as we shared ideas about the importance of the teaching process, and brainstormed about ways to generate productive discussion, their classes began to take off.

Both for those TAs precepting for me, and for others in the seminar, I emphasize concentrating on the literature students have read itself, rather than bringing in additional reading or criticism. Graduate students find this restriction very hard at first. They are worried that there will not be enough to say about the texts themselves, and they are used to thinking about content, and about mastering critical opinion. But the precept is the only time the students have to discuss the book together – an hour or so a week, divided among 10–15 of them. This is not the time for the instructor to lecture or add content.

Despite my pleas, however, virtually none of the TAs could resist adding content, assigning critical essays, or lecturing about theory. When we read Nick Hornby's *High Fidelity*, one recommended Walter Benjamin's "Unpacking My Library" for a discussion on "collecting and what it means culturally – Marxism lite." On *The Handmaid's Tale*, another had them "compare the Commander's rationale with a paragraph from a review of Susan Faludi's new book on male anomie (*Stiffed*)." Another "ended up explaining that May Day is a term for a fertility festival, which led me to telling them about carnival, the Shakespearean 'green world' and its significance for narrative structure." Sometimes the lecture-digression became longer than they had anticipated: "I started with what I meant to be a 90-second explanation of Augustine and predestined salvation. In fact it became more than that, and we got to Manicheanism and original sin and so on." And they underestimated how much time in general could be taken up by their own special interests. On Wilde, "We discussed Lord Henry's seduction of Dorian. I gave a little riff on Plato: disembodied desire, spiritual (pro)creation, initiation models of sex/tutelage." Or on Atwood, "I used some references to Havel's thought on dissidence within a totalitarian state (how dissidence is structurally necessary to totalitarianism) and threw in a reference to Zizek's 'obscene nightly law' because it seemed really helpful." Or on Angela Carter, "I was surprised that none of my students had read the Marquis de Sade."

These were exciting classes for graduate students who loved sharing their ideas and for undergraduates who got to hear graduate students model a sophisticated and enthusiastic approach to reading literature; but we had to think too about the point when such explanations could overpower student response, and when an ostensible open "discussion" was becoming an obliquely-directed argument. Often the TAs made these discoveries themselves: "I think I gave them too much guff on postmodernism (Eco and Zizek) – I got a bit carried away." Or on Ishiguro, "I found myself talking too much about passages where Stevens says his father 'embodied dignity,' my eventual point being that butlers have no bodies, so they can only 'embody' dignity and crying is a lapse. Needless to say, I started to sound very, very silly to myself and realized that my march towards a thesis on butlers and disembodied labor was not finding sympathetic Marxist revolutionary ears." In an American literature class on Zane Grey, a TA brought in a handout with quotations from Whitman, Emerson, and Thoreau "which deflated the class energy markedly. I ended up guiding them to my concerns and although they didn't exactly resent it, it was hardly the most sterling moment of the semester. How could it have been produced without compromising the group energy so markedly?"

In contrast, TAs found discussions really taking off when students had the chance to brainstorm and build on each others' ideas. "I said, Everyone talks about what Kurtz means – so just shout out, what is 'the horror' for you?" And it got going immediately. I wrote "the horror" on the board, and added their suggestions. Then people started pointing out connections and corrections." "I think the trick is for me to start softly softly with the way they see things, and walk slowly and secretly into uncharted territory." "We talked about the ending, and I made them vote on whether it was optimistic or pessimistic. They were mostly optimistic, but discussion was very heated." "I learned a great lesson about letting go of control over content and having faith in serendipity and process, student creativity, and letting the discussion take its own course." "Today I began by asking 'Why does this book take so long to read? Why is it so difficult?' and this turned out to be the best strategy yet in my experience. They had tons of really interesting questions and talked more to each other than to me."

The hardest thing for TAs to learn was how to pursue student comments with questions, and to get to deeper levels of discussion without lecturing. Martin Bickman, who has taught a pedagogy seminar for graduate students, says that his students worried about what might happen if the undergraduates became "too diffuse, too anecdotal, too digressive? At one point, we handled our feelings about this by agreeing to mentally allot each class period one ten-minute bullshit quota in the interests of keeping the discussions lively and unimpeded. But as we analyzed the classes, it became clear that one person's bullshit is another's insight." They gradually understood that "what may seem banal or obvious for the professor who may have passed this way decades ago and forgotten his or her own learning processes may need to be stated, clarified, reiterated, explicated by undergraduates for each other."[8]

116

Rather than offering my own syllabus for a teaching seminar, I have organized some of our postings into categories that you may use as case studies in your own literary pedagogy workshops. In the case-study method, we read the narrative, and then talk about what the teacher should do. (In more complex case studies, there are stages of revealing more detail about follow-up, with further discussion and analysis). What deeper issues and problems does the situation in the case call to mind?

Beginning

(1) Nerves got the best of me, and while I introduced myself, gave them info on how to contact me, and explained how available I was for discussion, problems, etc., I FORGOT TO ASK THEM TO INTRODUCE THEMSELVES!

(2) I started this class by venturing to the blackboard, my first time, and something that caused a stir.

(3) As always I suffered a bit from nervousness that makes me talk too quickly and start talking before students have time to think and answer. I definitely have a bit of the old fear of silence we talked about in our teaching seminar. I tried to count to five, but I only made it to two!

(4) As usual, I felt like I knew the issues that were useful to discuss; I had already taught the book and garnered some ideas about what worked and what didn't. Also Thursday mornings are devoted to my own research. So I arrived in the room with tons of papers and books in my bookbag, and my teaching notes were under these papers and I pulled everything out and set it on the desk. Whoa – here was the teacher with reams and reams of pages; if I had been in the course I would have been completely intimidated. I'm embarrassed to say that 8 of the 16 students did not contribute, even once.

(5) *What happened:*
Lesson one: be prepared. My first precept on Wednesday – I wanted to review the syllabus to make sure we were all on the same schedule. But I hadn't brought the syllabus. I dug through my bag bringing out disused graph paper, lip balm, month-old notes, and month-old phone bills.
What he did:
It was all a little embarrassing, but I borrowed a copy, and my disorganization paved the way for a casual discussion of how to

117

organize thoughts about a dense novel. We surveyed the options –
post-its, dog-ears, photographic memory. My own method is a low-
tech one: when I start to notice an interesting pattern, I track the
page numbers on the back flap. The problem with this method is
that you often miss the first instances of a recurring theme.

These comments were all about the implicit teaching contract TAs felt they
were setting in their behavior, rather than their words. What should they
have done next, or what do you think of what they did do next? Are these
trivial issues? What kind of teaching persona is being established in each case?

Opening Questions

(1)   An acquaintance of mine once opened a class with the question,
      "Who in here knows anything about seventeenth-century Biblical
      textual scholarship?"

(2)   It's funny, sometimes you think you have a really thought-
      provoking question that will lead to a lengthy discussion. You
      throw the question out and one person kind of hazards a response
      and then there is dead silence. It's hard to know what will get people
      going.

(3)   I came in with the opening questions, "Were you struck by the
      number of naval mutinies in the text? Did you find it strange that
      nearly every ship that arrives on the coast of Africa has just had a
      mutiny?" But it became clear to me that although the class agreed
      they were surprised by the number of mutinies, they didn't want to
      pursue this any further. Any explanation?

(4)   Although we discussed the importance of the opening question
      several weeks ago, it was not until this week's precepts that I really
      experienced the effects of the opening minutes of the entire class.
      The lesson came from the student presentations delivered this week
      and defied my expectations thoroughly . . . Essentially, Monday's
      presentation tended towards the "raising questions" model and gen-
      erated remarkable class participation and engagement; Tuesday's
      presentation (which I initially considered better) made specific argu-
      ments about the specific portions of the text – and everybody shut
      up so thoroughly it took nearly 45 minutes to get them talking
      again.

118

(5) I asked them to decide what age the speaker is in Shakespeare's Sonnet #146, and then say how they could tell. How would the message change if the speaker's age were different?

How should the teacher kick off a class discussion? What kinds of questions are best at the beginning of a discussion?

Controlling the Discussion

(1) My mini-crisis is this – I go into the class with a lesson plan, because I believe that there are key issues that need to be discussed. I pitch these issues as very broad questions that lead to what I think are the key moments of the text. I also try to get their own personal reactions to things, though I think this is secondary. I don't take the "touchy-feely" approach to lit. I'm more of an issues person. And the students are talking up a storm. Yet I'm wondering, based on my conversations with others, if I'm pushing my own agenda. Could we all talk about this?

(2) I had a very detailed and carefully timed plan going into the first precept. It involved changes of subject every 25 or 30 minutes, a short writing project at 75 minutes, etc. Very little of it actually materialized.

(3) I tried to talk about postcolonialism and they were all resolutely uninterested. I tried everything from my own childhood to asking if they had read Garcia Marquez, but they were skeptical and I think felt preached at.

(4) Strangely enough, my efforts to foreground the question of misogyny brought forward a motley assortment of protestations and defenses.

(5) This class was far more inclined to like Alex (*Clockwork Orange*) and largely believed his will to have a son was an altruistic and "natural" one. And I chickened out of talking about homosexuality.

(6) I put some dates on the board and tried to get the students to note instabilities within the novel in terms of social class, race, economics, politics, etc. I got all these issues on the table, but I had the feeling that I was dragging the students through these big

issues, albeit rooting them in the novel, and that they became fairly passive.

(7)   I had 30 minutes left and nothing else to ask them about. They had covered the topics they brought up in their email. We had covered all the questions I had prepared and looked at every passage that was at all interesting. When I asked them if they had any questions or things they wanted to discuss about the earlier reading they didn't. They made a valiant effort to keep the discussion going but it was clear to all of us that it was foundering. I let them go ten minutes early because I couldn't think what else to do.

(8)   Out of the thin air of those clichés, it occurred to me that the girls' bonding conversation had often used the sort of phrases that linguists call phatic – those things like "How are you?" and "What's up?" that don't carry any real semantic content but just affirm that lines of conversation are open. I thought that attaching the word phatic to this small epiphany would ruin it, but the students just grabbed it and ran. First one used the term, then someone else. Soon everyone was talking about the phatic elements in their own interactions, and springing from that to the language used between characters in the book, and by Moore, as narrator, herself.

(9)   I started by asking them to break into groups of three and list all the literary citations Chanticleer uses in order to make his argument about paying attention to our dreams. This worked very well. They were very into it; the room was buzzing and they were leafing through the text and writing furiously. I liked this exercise both because it broke the ice and got them talking to each other, and because it grounded the following discussion very securely in the text. I then asked them analytical questions about the first list – What categories do these citations fall into? Why does Chanticleer use them? Do they prove his case effectively?

(10)   I am concerned about handling gender issues well in this class. I fear shutting the male voices down because I know that I tend to look all excited and happy when students approach literature with my own (feminist) point of view. Not, obviously, that men can't be feminists and that some jerks deserve shutting down.

(11)   I froze. I panicked. I didn't employ the lessons learned from our case study! Remember the scenario in which the student claims Nazi atrocities didn't occur and the political tension in the class-

room skyrockets? Well, while discussing *Gone with the Wind*, one of my white Southern students declared that she had been raised to use the "n-word," and thought overly sensitive northerners who were raised in rich white enclaves had no right to condemn her. I wasn't sure what to do, so I took the easiest way out and ignored her declaration. I'm curious to hear what the rest of you would have done.

How much should the teacher plan and guide the discussion? What is the best way to introduce and handle controversial topics? How forthright should the teacher be about his or her own position or standpoint? When can in-class writing get us over some plateaus?

Course Planning, Pacing, and Continuity

(1) They have been having some difficulties following the characters and the episodes. I hadn't anticipated the degree on plot review they showed signs of needing. We ended up clarifying plot and characters only in the context of discussing particular passages or when students asked a specific question. I now realize it would have been more helpful to start each class with at least a ten-minute summary of what we'd read – in fact a student later suggested that we should have done this. The truly helpful thing would be to give them each a xerox of my *Cliffs Notes* on *The Faerie Queene*, but I can see that for several reasons this is not an option.

(2) I think jumping from Milton to Pope in a course that was supposed to be historically oriented was difficult. The semester has definitely given me food for thought on the subjects of effective syllabus design and the purpose of survey courses.

(3) I've been getting better at planning a realistic number of passages/texts to discuss, which allows me to plan better for themes and questions and possible conclusions. It's no longer surprising to me that one sonnet plus two 20-line passages from *Paradise Lost* can take up two hours (at least, with all the amount of hand-wringing and hand-waving we do).

(4) My precepts were on *The Woman in White*. It is a 650-page novel and I hoped they would have made it through the first half. By the end of the first precept I realized I was vastly mistaken and found myself getting annoyed at my students.

121

(5) They were supposed to come extra-prepared. When they seemed unwilling/unable to respond to anything for a solid 30 minutes I just got fed up. This was painful, to the point where I gave them a mini-lecture about preparation which was probably counter-productive. I will say that afterward we did a close reading of the deathbed scene, and they were all making an effort. In the end, we covered adequate territory, but it was like pulling teeth.
What should the TA do in the next class meeting?

How much should students be expected to read? How much to discuss? How do we mediate between historical breadth and textual depth? How do we motivate students to keep up with the reading?

Classroom Management

(1) I have two of what McKeachie calls "Dominators." I have two male students, who always sit at the front, one on either side of me! One a little too close, as I don't like to have students peering at my notes. Yet the section is huge so someone has to sit that close. They are very confident and ready to make eye contact and respond quickly and at length to my questions. I try to stare past them to some of the less voluble members of the section, but I fear I am often caught in the crossfire of these two gentlemen's eager looks and interjections.

(2) One thing that really disturbs me is that the silent ones were pre-dominantly the women in the class. Having gone to a women's college myself, I'm profoundly disturbed to find that I am creating an environment in which the women hang back and let the men take over the discussion. Any thoughts on how to rectify this?

(3) *What happened:*
I have one student who is falling into the silent role. Last week I asked her to read out a passage, but this week I thought it would be too obvious to do that again, so I asked her directly what she thought on a particular topic. She just glared at me and didn't speak and another student came to her rescue.
What the TA did:
I emailed her afterward and said I hoped she didn't mind my calling on her, but I thought that sometimes it was hard to get into

the discussion and I wanted to give her a chance to speak. She responded immediately, saying that she agreed it was hard to get into the discussion and she was just taken by surprise when I called on her.
What should the TA do next?

(4) One particularly gruesome moment for me was when I noticed one student nodding off. I resisted the urge to tell him after class to buy himself a weekly pre-precept cup of coffee. Maybe I should have. What would you all have done?

(5) This precept is completely uninspired and uninspirational. I feel that the students are getting short-changed in a way because the discussions are much better in other precepts. Maybe I need to have a more rigid lesson-plan and just force-feed them.

(6) The student just kept going and going and going. She gave what turned out to be a comprehensive examination of all the illustrations of various editions of *Little Women* from 1868 to the present, set up beautifully on her computer. At 25 minutes I sensed some restlessness among the other students and began to get really nervous because no end appeared to be in sight. I quietly asked her to speed up a little because we were running out of time and wouldn't get a chance to talk about what she was showing us. She readily complied and flew through her material but still took another fifteen minutes. I don't really know how I should have handled the situation.

Among the problems raised by these comments is whether the teacher should try to have everyone speak. Martin Bickman says yes: "One learns more by articulating than just absorbing. Even students who spoke only once or twice a class seemed to be more engaged than those who try to be just bystanders."[9] How should we handle students who talk too much, students who talk too little, students who fall asleep?

Ending

We read *Harry Potter and the Sorceror's Stone*, which the students had chosen by overwhelming majority as the last text of the semester. I had the students write down the overarching themes of the course, and then try to fit Harry Potter into them. They liked the cumulative aspect, which helped them think about the course as a whole rather than in 12 isolated parts.

Grading

(1)   What grade to give a paper whose only flaw is that it is uninteresting?

(2)   One of my students picked up his paper after precept. It was a C+. He was really angry and aggressive. "I mean, what is this? I read all these books, I go to precept, and you give a C+ because you say I've got no structure?" He started whacking the paper and asking me what structure I wanted. I asked him to come meet with me, and that this was only an intermediate grade, but he laughed bitterly and went away.

Student Course Evaluations

In all my precepts I had them write little evaluations, asking them what things they liked and things they didn't, and I encouraged them to make suggestions drawn from other precepts – things we didn't do they might enjoy, etc. I got some great feedback.

All of us will have our own ideas and prejudices about what makes a teacher good, and whether it can be taught. In my workshop I had one British TA who found "much of the self-help stuff embarrassingly personal or touchy-feely," and another TA who felt that teaching was so intimate and personal that it could not be analyzed. Jerome McGann, who experimented with a seminar for graduate students on the teaching of fiction, concluded that it ended up being more about problems than solutions. But he concluded that "critical reflection about the problems" had to be undertaken.[10] I strongly agree. "Developing as a teacher," Kenneth Eble writes, "can be described as becoming wiser and less judgmental, more generous, less arrogant and yet more confident; being more honest with oneself and students and subject matter; taking more risks; showing forth without showing off; being impatient with ignorance but not appalled with it. These attributes are partly matters of personal development, but they are not unrelated to learning teaching techniques, acquiring knowledge, and expanding one's professional range."[11]

Chapter 9
Teaching Dangerous Subjects

When American teachers of literature think about controversial, dangerous, or explosive subjects, they are likely to think first of race. Given the centrality and sensitivity of racial issues in the United States, and the vigorous protests that have been made against the cultural monuments, symbols, and canons that some believe perpetuate racist ideology, few teachers would embark on teaching *Huckleberry Finn* or *Native Son* without consideration of the racially and emotionally charged language, events, and themes in these books. In a book about teaching Mark Twain, the editor's first question is "How can a teacher successfully deal with the more than two hundred occurrences of various forms of the word 'nigger' in *Huckleberry Finn* and with Twain's portrayal of the slave Jim (at times) in accordance with some of the most demeaning of nineteenth-century stereotypes for African Americans? Should these aspects of the novel disqualify it from being taught? Or can they be turned to pedagogical advantage?"[1] Discussing Richard Wright's novel, teachers comment that occasionally a "hypermasculine white reader . . . is so threatened by Bigger Thomas that he may storm out," that "black male students are deeply torn in their responses to *Native Son*," and that women students react with anger to Wright's misogyny.[2]

Similarly, when Isobel Armstrong taught postcolonial and African literature in a course called "Women at the Margins," the classroom "exploded with pain and violence." She had to "reintegrate the class with discussion, and especially historical and cultural contexts." Teaching black literature in Britain, she says, "is always explosive because it's dark times all the time.

West Indian students are very much in conflict over the use of standard English."

But the awareness literature teachers bring to representations of race, dialect, and ethnicity does not usually extend to the many other difficult subjects literature presents, and sometimes romanticizes, such as suicide, abortion, pornography and sexually graphic language, drug addiction, and alcoholism. Because we have become accustomed to treating the material as fictional or textual, teachers can overlook the sensitivity of content.

One important principle is candor and clear labeling – telling students in advance that they may be offended or upset; contextualizing the topic with some sociological or historical background; being prepared for some students to be shocked or upset no matter what you do, and allowing opportunities for them to respond. In "Syllabuses of Risk," Jeffrey Berman recommends that literature teachers should alert students to the potentially depressive effect of some of the books we study, "just as physicians and pharmacists routinely inform their patients of possible adverse reactions to a drug." Berman stresses that he does not mean we should "avoid asking students to read emotionally charged texts, but that we need to give more thought to how we do so."[3] I tell graduate students in my teaching seminar to ask themselves what they would *wish* to have said in class if a student subsequently reacted badly to a book, and to go ahead and say it.

Suicide

The most dangerous of the dangerous subjects is suicide. Many important literary works deal with suicide – *Madame Bovary, Anna Karenina, The Awakening, Mrs. Dalloway, The Bell Jar, Hedda Gabler, Miss Julie* – and many writers – Hemingway, Virginia Woolf, Sylvia Plath, Anne Sexton, John Berryman – were themselves suicidal. Kaye Redfield Jamison, a specialist on adolescent suicides, points out that the suicide rate among young people has tripled in the past half century. As professors of literature, we are thus teaching the highest demographic risk group for suicide.

An important book dealing with this problem is Jeffrey Berman's *Surviving Literary Suicide*. Berman raises the significant and too-rarely-asked questions about the ethics of teaching this particular theme: "Literature is filled with countless numbers of suicidal characters, many of whom are studied every day in high schools and colleges, without any discussion of how their deaths affect readers. Does a fictional character's suicide awaken the same emotions within us as a real character's suicide? What are the conditions in which a reader's identification with a suicidal character may lead

126

to heightened vulnerability? In an age when the suicide rate has jumped dramatically, does a story's glorification of suicide pose special dangers to readers? If so, can we identify those who may be at risk and take appropriate measures to avert a tragedy?"[4]

Berman believes that "literature teachers can play a vital role in suicide prevention, for they are often the first to realize from a diary or personal essay that a student may be depressed." In my own teaching experience, this has certainly been the case. But what should we do? Often "teachers are reluctant to discuss the subject, even when they teach suicidal literature. Teachers' silence may reflect the widespread myth that talking or writing about suicide will heighten a student's vulnerability." Moreover, while some university health centers are open and pro-active about discussing mental health issues and prevention, others are bound by rules of confidentiality and habits of silence. Many years ago, I called the university counseling service to discuss a student I was sure was suicidal, to be told brusquely on the phone, "Well, *you* seem very upset." It took all my persistence to keep insisting on information about what to do next. In that case, I knew the student's personal background, and was able to talk to him about his feelings. Avoiding or evading his comments about suicide could have made things worse, since, as Berman points out, "teachers are not trained to be therapists, but they inadvertently confirm the stigma attached to suicide by avoiding appropriate discussions."[5]

Berman points out other problems in teaching "novels and poems by authors who later take their own lives . . . Given what clinicians call the contagion effect – suicide's ability to 'infect' other people, rendering them susceptible to self-death – should literature teachers take special precautions when discussing self-destructive authors?"[6] Diane Middlebrook teaches Sylvia Plath and Anne Sexton, and knows how seductive these poets can be to adolescents. She believes that "the professor must take responsibility for leading a discussion about suicide. I ask how many ways are there of thinking about these metaphors? In poetry, suicide is a trope, a way of thinking about feelings. In life, it is a form of mental illness, a bi-polar pathology. I have them read sections from Kay Jamison's book on suicide."

When I teach a book like *The Bell Jar* or *The Virgin Suicides*, I try to educate and inform students about suicide, and distribute a handout about how they can intervene if a friend seems depressed or suicidal.[7] In one class precept about Eugenides' novel, a TA asked the students "whether the boys could have prevented the tragedy if they had read the handout on intervention. I was disturbed and saddened by the consistent response: no." Another TA reported that "one woman, her voice and body trembling, opined that she found Cecilia's suicide so 'traumatizing' that she could hardly bear to read beyond it. I valorized her right to have such an emotional and intellectual reaction, but I left to her peers the problems of how to channel her contribution and how to help with her anxieties. Responses were very sophisticated, careful, and caring. Several of the women students drew her attention to matters structural, suggesting that Eugenides stages Cecilia's death when and how he does to comment on society's response to the phenomenon of female teenage suicide. We moved on to consider the ethics/morality of writing an erotically and comically inflected book on this sensitive subject."

Explicit Sexual Language

When I started teaching, Victorian literature was almost the only literary period free from sexually explicit language. Now, perhaps in rebellion, Victorianists have become notorious for our interest in sexuality. The norms of linguistic acceptance change rapidly from Clark Gable's taboo-breaking utterance, "Frankly, Scarlet, I don't give a damn." in *Gone with the Wind* (1939) to Erica Jong's "zipless fuck" in *Fear of Flying* (1971) to the rappers and punk novelists of the twenty-first century. Today's undergraduates will have heard every form of obscenity uttered over a laugh track on television, or spoken in the movies, or accessed on computers. The contemporary novels deal with every sexual scenario imaginable from love between humans and bears or dolphins, to sex with raw liver or a dead chicken. Elizabeth Benedict, in her wonderful book, *The Joy of Writing Sex*, gives four criteria for a good sex scene:

1. It's "not always about good sex" but always about good writing.
2. It "connects to the larger concerns of the work."
3. It is driven by the "needs, impulses, and histories" of the characters.
4. It is about the relationship between the characters.[8]

In London, the *Literary Review* awards an annual Bad Sex Prize for the most dire scene in a novel. In 2001, it was presented by model Jerry Hall, who drawled that usually her response to bad sex was divorce papers. Jonathan Franzen, the Pulitzer-Prize winning author of *The Corrections*, was among the finalists for a scene in which a young man performs oral sex with a sofa. Oprah approved of the sofa scene enough to make this novel one of her Book Club choices.

But many literature teachers would find it awkward to discuss this scene in a classroom. The acceptable standards of discussing or even quoting explicit sexual language in poetry, plays, and fiction varies considerably from nation to nation, state to state, region to region, city to town. What should the professor do about sexually explicit language in literature? Skip it in a lecture? Use euphemisms? Condemn it? Should teachers of poetry emulate the genteel compositors who allegedly bowdlerized Philip Larkin's poem to read: "They tuck you up, your mum and dad"? Obviously, what might be scandalous in Scranton will be anodyne in Ann Arbor. Some teachers will work in colleges or even universities where explicit language can get them accused of sexual harassment, or even fired. They know who they are. But most English departments will simply ignore this question in their guidelines for faculty.

I believe that the professor's behavior and tone are crucial in shaping students' attitudes towards sexual language. If we are embarrassed, they will be embarrassed. If we are salacious, they will leer. Nonetheless, especially for women professors, sexual language and material can be problematic. I try to demystify and legitimize sexually explicit language in the classroom by using it in lecture, when reading passages from the text, without fuss or emphasis. Ann Thompson usually discusses the issue of gender and "obscenity" in Shakespeare with her students. In her work on editions of *Hamlet* she discovered that not until the late 1980s did editors annotating the "country matters" scene actually print the word "cunt." Previously they had referred coyly to "double entendre" and "sexual innuendo."

Those of us who teach in universities where sexual terminology and subject matter is accepted as part of the legitimate province of higher education will probably nonetheless discover that there are other dangers or border lines in the material. Lisa Jardine prepares her students for sexually graphic material, such as a video clip on the transformation scene for the film *The Crying Game* that she shows along with discussion of *Twelfth Night*. But she has had more difficulty with "the decorum of faith," and the anxieties of religious students and their parents about what is being taught. Michael Cadden has no problems teaching the plays of David Mamet, but has had objections to the homosexual language of Tony Kushner's *Angels in America*. One of my TA's felt "great anxiety about teaching [Lorrie Moore's novel] *Who Will Run the Frog Hospital* because of the ability of abortion as a subject to polarize a classroom and cause all kinds of unpleasantness. Friends and I have had terrible experiences assigning *Roe v. Wade*, etc. as topics in composition courses." When she taught the book, "My *Frog Hospital* precepts were overwhelmingly sad. I actually saw one student blinking hard, another trembling set of lips, and heard several hard swallows."

Some teachers may feel that any acknowledgment of the controversial nature of these issues is uncool or giving into censorship and repression.

129

Teachers of sociology, psychology, and law, among others, however, know that they have to be careful and thoughtful in introducing controversial and emotionally-charged subjects into the classroom. Martha Nussbaum points out that "many courses in criminal law do not address rape for precisely this reason, and those that do exercise special care to promote a sensitive atmosphere in the classroom."[9] Literature professors should not feel like wimps if they do the same.

Chapter 10
Teaching Literature in Dark Times

I've come to realize that the classroom is a microcosm of the world; it is the chance we have to practice whatever ideals we may cherish.
Jane Tompkins, *"Pedagogy of the Distressed"*

What should teachers do in the classroom in times of crisis, disaster, tragedy, sorrow, and panic? Does teaching literature, rather than economics or physics, demand that we rise to these occasions, and if so, how? In dark times, moments of personal or collective anguish, literature professors have to think about the abstractions of professional ethics in a much more urgent and existential way. At these moments, the clichés of our field suddenly take on startling life, and the platitudes of the humanities become credos that confront us with real choices and decisions on how to act.

Moreover, such moments must and will come within every professional teaching career. All of us will face some private or personal crisis during our lifetime as teachers – divorce, illness, family problems, the death of a parent or a friend. And all of us must expect to have to confront public crises and shared disasters in the classroom, from the death of a student or a colleague, to national emergencies. I have taught during the JFK and other assassinations, urban riots, the Cambodia invasion, the hostage crisis, Three-Mile Island, the Challenger explosion, the Gulf War, and the OJ trial verdict, among others.

Yet there is no public discussion of the moral, ethical, and practical dimensions of pedagogy in such times. As in so many circumstances, we make it

131

up as we go along; and we take our clues about how to behave from litera-ture and movies rather than from real discussions or debates with colleagues. In periods of past crisis, some critics did think deeply about the connections between their moral obligations as citizens and as teachers. Louise Rosenblatt, who wrote her classic work *Literature as Exploration* in 1938 under the shadow of fascism, insists that "the teaching of literature inevitably involves the conscious or unconscious reinforcement of ethical attitudes. It is practically impossible to treat . . . any literary work of art in a vital manner without confronting some problem of ethics and without speaking out of the context of some social philosophy." Rosenblatt believes that the teacher of literature should not assume "a mask of unemotional objectivity or impar-tial omniscience."[1]

On the whole, however, the bland contemporary material on the ethics of teaching avoids really difficult circumstances. In *The Elements of Teaching*, for example, James M. Banner and Harold Cannon say only that "in teach-ing, ethics means putting the satisfaction of the needs and good of students before those of anyone else."[2] In other guidebooks, "ethics" refers only to fair grades. Wilbert McKeachie is unusual in his forthright commitment to values in teaching. "In fact," he writes, "I argue that we can't avoid teach-ing values . . . Our choices of content, our choices of teaching methods, our very ways of conducting classes reveal our values and influence our students' reactions."[3]

One traditional view of the professor's responsibility is sticking to the syl-labus and going on with business as usual, with the explanation that the normal routine is the best behavior in crisis, and an affirmation of the intel-lect against panic. In other words, the "Mr. Chips" model. In James Hilton's best-seller of 1934 about a classics teacher at Brookfield, a British boys' school during World War I, there is an air-raid while Chips is taking the lower fourth in Latin. As the guns and anti-aircraft shells roar and the shrapnel falls, Chips endearingly goes on with his lesson: "If it is fate that we are soon to be – umph – interrupted, let us be found employing ourselves in some-thing – umph – really appropriate? Is there anyone who will volunteer to construe?" As it happens, the passage they are reading in Caesar's Gallic Wars deals with the Germans, and Chips remarks: "Well – umph – you can see – now – that these dead languages – umph – can come to life again – some-times." Afterwards, "they found that five bombs had fallen in and around Brookfield, the nearest of them just outside the School grounds. Nine persons had been killed." Chips' phlegm becomes a legend and he becomes a "symbol of victory."[4]

Of course, we might think today that Chips would have been wiser to evacuate the classroom. What did literature professors really do under fire?

Literature both seems irrelevant in tragedy and crucial in its power to console and illuminate. In 1915, in the midst of the Great War, the president of the MLA, Jefferson Fletcher, reflected that the catastrophic times would bring some reward to European scholars tested by suffering: "When the teachers and scholars who may survive, go back to classrooms and study, they must bring with them some spirit of the open – and of the deeps. That tragic sense of life, to which they have been recalled, must, it seems, cleanse their minds of the dry-rot of pedantry and the mildew of dilettantism . . . We in our fat peace have the leisure, the money, the trained men, but can we surely contest with Europe's remnant of scholars the deepened insight and the strengthened will?"[5]

In the turmoil of the 1960s and 1970s, many literature professors had to confront the disparity between their subject and what was going on outside the classroom. Jyl Lynn Felman recalls the effects on the country when John F. Kennedy was shot: "Teachers dropped the yellow chalk in their hands, stopped algebra lessons in the middle, or abruptly ended the class discussion on *The Old Man and the Sea*. They started sobbing hysterically right in front of their students, as the news that the President of the United States of America had been shot and killed came piping into the classroom . . . Classes were immediately dismissed." Felman uses her childhood memories as model of what should happen in the classroom when "there is an intellectual crisis of pedagogical importance. Regular programming is interrupted as the pre-planned lesson is dropped. The professor is forced to stop. She must attend to the spectacle unfolding in front of her, and the spectacular outpouring of emotion coming from the students instantaneously turned spectators . . . The spectacle can come from the outside, as in the O.J. Simpson verdict, or it can originate organically and unintentionally, as a consequence of the class material itself. Either way, the spectacle must be confronted; spectacles will not be ignored."[6]

Carolyn Shrodes, for, example, had an experience during a class at San Francisco State during the Cambodian invasion in May 1970: "On the first of those tragic days in early May, before some of our classes had been 'reconstituted,' the emergency alarm shattered the peace of the Humanities Building as we were discussing the influence of Blake on Yeats in English 186. In disciplined silence we filed out into the quad . . . Rumor had it that this time a bomb had been planted, not in the despised quarters of ROTC but in the heretofore inviolable citadel of humanities, language, and literature. In twenty minutes the safe-return bell sounded. As if nothing had happened, we tried to resume our academic discussion. But the reverberations of the strident alarm continued, echoing the warning cries from the campuses of Kent, Jackson and Augusta. We were no longer in the world of

Blake and Yeats."[7] In student street riots in Korea in the 1980s, professors told Hyungji Park, "tear gas and Molotov cocktails would explode outside the classroom windows . . . while inside we lectured on symbolism in T. S. Eliot's poetry."[8]

While Mr. Chips seems to be in one kind of denial, these professors testify that academia continued to be in denial of another kind, even less in touch with the emotions of their students and the relevance of their texts. The message of the sixties was that national crisis should be met by political action or semi-political organizing, *outside* the classroom. The protest petition, the teach-in, the conference, the resolution for the Delegate Assembly of the MLA, even the strike, were all responses developed during the Vietnam War. Jerry Aline Flieger recalls a day "in 1969 or 1970 . . . when a rock came sailing through my classroom window at Berkeley. I was a new teaching assistant, conducting a class in beginning French, mildly interested by the uprising on the Berkeley campus about ROTC recruiting on campus – interested, sympathetic, but as yet uninvolved. And then, the rock was pitched through my window, my classroom was invaded by three young men who announced that the university was on strike, and who demanded that we dismiss class and join them. We did – out of solidarity? Or embarrassment? – but this incident in any case was a dividing line in my life, marking my first real involvement in anti-war protests, or in protest of any kind."[9]

The message of the eighties was that literature itself was political, and that external crises could be countered by pointing to the racist or sexist or postcolonial subtexts of the syllabus. Missing in both of these responses was a reflection on teaching itself as a humane, humanistic, value-laden art. In my view, there are two kinds of crisis teachers of literature face in the classroom. The first is when we ourselves have been personally hit by loss or tragedy, suffered our own illness, or the illness and death of those we love. In my experience, teaching as usual is the best we can do for ourselves in these situations, and sticking to the task, the routine, and the text offers a kind of concentration and forgetfulness of self that can be a relief from our own anxieties. Stuart Sherman writes that "the absorptions of the class hour can offer safe haven from ordinary suffering, even from extraordinary. I have known teachers mortally ill who forget their dying when lost in the crossplay of class discussion."[10] During the week before I had major exploratory surgery, I was grateful for the classroom, and found it almost the only place where I could stop worrying about myself. In addition, dumping our woes on our students, whether the pain of an illness or an ongoing divorce, is never a good idea. Stoicism at these private moments is its own best reward.

But when the tragedy is general and public and collective, when students too are caught up in uncertainty, grief, and fear, our task is much more complicated. These are the times that test our claims that literature teaches us how to be human, simple, and kind, as Margaret Edson suggests in her Pulitzer-Prize-winning play *W;t*, whose terminally-ill English professor heroine rethinks her scholarship in the face of death: "Now is not the time for verbal swordplay, for unlikely flights of imagination and wildly shifting perspectives, for metaphysical conceit, for wit. And nothing would be worse than a detailed scholarly analysis. Erudition. Interpretation. Complication . . . Now is a time for simplicity. Now is a time for, dare I say it, kindness."

American academics faced a major moral and emotional challenge on September 11, 2001, when the World Trade Center and the Pentagon were attacked, and even more so in the confusing days that followed. Reactions during the fall of September 2001, by readers and teachers, showed how vulnerable our assumptions about the usefulness of literature were, but also how meaningful it can be to rise to an occasion with all our skills and learning and expertise. Teaching during this dark time was also a template for the varieties of academic belief. Lisa Ruddick, at the University of Chicago, reported that many scholars had discovered "that the challenge of meeting their traumatized students on some shared human ground has evoked some of the most meaningful encounters of the teaching life," while a graduate student was asking herself, "if you're not getting at anything that sustains people, *what's the point?*"[11] On the opposite extreme, some resisted any suggestion that they should try to sustain people. One distinguished teacher, a woman I respect, told me firmly that "we are not in the consolation business." Another English department quickly organized a conference on the burning topic of "literary theory after September 11."

Vijay Seshadri, a poet who teaches at Sarah Lawrence, went through several stages in his scheduled discussion of Whitman. Initially, he wanted to get his freshman poetry class back to work on "Song of Myself." "I went into my Monday class," he wrote, "thinking that we had already lost the previous Thursday's discussion to confusion and grief and talk that went nowhere, and that we had to turn back to the demands of my schedule." But his students were defiantly resistant to Whitman, despite his intense efforts to win them over to its spiritual vision. He taught the poem again to a graduate class at Columbia, and read from Whitman at a New York memorial. But only gradually did he come to realize that his own emotions had been transferred to Whitman in an experience that was cathartic for him, but perhaps less meaningful for his students. "But seeing the poem the way I saw it helped me. It gave me a way to hold the event in my mind, to come closer to it, and not be afraid."[12]

The question is whether the teacher might have opened the seminar more to allow students to have their own responses to Whitman, or whether he needed to be flexible about the syllabus in the face of their hostility. Another professor reported that she stuck to the syllabus of her American literature seminar, and that she and the students were initially grateful for the comfort of routine and intellectual discipline. But by the second week, she noticed, concentration was wavering, and the students' distress was making itself felt in absences and lack of preparation.

Closer to the scene, such detachment was impossible; and the need to address the situation directly may have speeded the process of recovery. Faculty who confronted their classes and changed their syllabus in response to the situation reported that sympathy and reason were not at odds, but that expressing pain and suffering allowed thinking and recovery to take place as well. Trying to plan his first class on the day after the attack, for example, Douglas L. Howard, who runs the writing center at Suffolk County Community College in Long Island, reflected upon the values he had internalized: "Professionalism generally upholds the importance of the job over personal concerns. In spite of whatever feelings you might be experiencing or distractions you might be facing, the job always takes precedence, and personal preoccupations should always take a backseat to performance and the task at hand." But in this emergency, he felt, there were other values to consider as well: "We are not automatons, and in certain situations we need to give voice to our pain and suffering, to show our students that academic development is as much about sympathy, empathy, and insight as it is about reason, hypothesis, and deduction."[13]

Howard had been planning to teach about "the instability of the narrator in Edgar Allan Poe's *Ligeia*, but how could I talk to the students about his instability after what had happened, after all we had just witnessed and experienced? The world of Poe seemed almost sane by comparison." In class, "instead of trying to lecture my students or dictate to them or ignore what we both were obviously feeling, I talked to them. And they talked to me. We talked about the images we had seen, the planes, the people, the damage, the rescue efforts. We talked about who might have done it and why. We wondered what would happen next. Some disagreed about how the United States should retaliate. And shortly thereafter, we returned to Poe."[14]

At the downtown campus of Pace University, two blocks from the World Trade Center, English professor Karla Jay, who had narrowly survived an apartment building fire in 1977, and who remembered the first bombing of the WTC in 1993, was wondering what to do when the university re-opened.

136

Her students had been evacuated, had seen the "towers implode and watched smoking bodies and body parts tumble from the sky." She herself was feeling the pain of post-traumatic stress: "I shook uncontrollably, was unable to sleep, and suffered from an upset stomach." She was unable to face traveling on the subway. "I am no hero, only a fragile survivor. How could I hope to be the strong arm around my students when I could not conquer my own terror?" But Jay did conquer it, and shakily took the A train to her campus for a workshop on how to help students to cope. "Though we were told that a range of emotions from shock and hysteria to anger were normal, we left without a clue about what to do if a student ran screaming from the room. For the first time in my teaching career, I went home and had a stiff drink."

Jay's process for coping with the emergency was a model for how we might think about our task in the future. First, she thought about what had been helpful in her own experiences as a student. "I remembered that when I was an undergraduate I had been caught up in the April 1968 uprisings at Columbia University, which shut the campus for at least 10 pivotal days before final exams. Several faculty members invited us into their homes to continue with our work. That gave us some continuity and also some assurance that our semester wouldn't be a washout." She contacted her literature students and told them that if Pace was closed for more than a week, they would meet at her home. She suggested that they should turn off the television and try to read their assignment, *Frankenstein*: "In some ways, there couldn't be a more apt text dealing with good and evil, creation and destruction, the desire to control human destiny, the failure to take responsibility for one's acts."

As she regained her own emotional control, Jay thought about the relevance of her teaching aims to the emergency. She encouraged her former creative-writing students to write about the event. She emailed students in her women's studies community service course urging them to continue their volunteer activities with children, the elderly, and AIDS patients. Her current sophomore-level women's literature course was more of a challenge. Typically, Jay notes, "I would approach Mary Shelley's *Frankenstein* from a feminist perspective . . . But I didn't feel that I could go into the class with a firm plan, nor could I reduce their education to a semester of therapy. I would steer a middle ground. I would have to see what shape the students were in and try to reach for issues that related to the events at large." Her first-generation students, many from the former Soviet Union, were exhausted but determined "not to let terrorism deprive them of an education . . . I thought I would have to hold them together; instead, they healed my soul."[15] Jay's solutions met one of the most important aspects of crisis teaching: getting the students to use their own knowledge and skills actively to come to terms with the situation.

One of the most shattering discoveries of teaching in tragedy is that literature does not invariably offer the solace and the wisdom we claim for it; and this discovery is part of the hard truth we must confront and explore. Carolyn Foster Segal, who teaches at Cedar Crest College, found her syllabus in modernist literature unbearably cruel and cold, as the Korean teachers did when they taught Eliot in the midst of riots: "My syllabuses for twentieth-century American literature seemed to be lists of grief and grievances . . . I want more – another category beyond those, beyond irony. I turn the pages of my anthology – mockeries of loss, museums of nothingness, without solace."[16]

William Germano, the vice-president of Routledge, polled his friends in the academy and publishing about what they were reading in the days after the attack. He himself, unable to concentrate on a novel, was re-reading an old Latin grammar – "it wasn't exactly like reading – it was more like a focalization exercise, the kind of thing some people do to shake off migraines" – at least until the exercises about the Gallic Wars came too close to reality. Unlike Mr. Chips, Germano did not find comfort in the historical analogs to violence.

Indeed, he reported, many others could not read anything except newspapers, email, and magazines. No one who did read a book was reading fiction. Among their choices were biographies, natural history, Buddhist self-help books, the Bible, American history, spiritual texts, travel literature, philosophy, manuals of household repair, Auden's poetry, Shakespeare's comedies. "This morning," said philosopher Arthur Danto, "I woke up from a dream in which I was acting in one of these plays, with cowslips (which I could not identify in waking life), brooks, and clowns. I felt very happy, but then with a crash the present world hit me, and I am back where I have been since it happened, housing this terrible cloud in my chest." Germano was troubled to discover that he had spent a week "away from books, unable to read even one."[17]

But others discovered that teaching literature provided them with a depth of tragic understanding they had never anticipated. Julie Crosby, a graduate student in medieval literature at Columbia, was teaching the "Great Books" course: "On the day of the attacks, we were supposed to finish Homer's *Iliad*. A mere 48 hours later, our oldest epic – a story of humans facing death and replacing anger with compassion – resonated with a profundity that I had never experienced in the classroom. This singular occasion made all previous student–teacher encounters seem superficial."[18]

Isobel Armstrong was at an academic conference in Tours on September 11, 2001, and the organizers felt they "had to go on – because terrorist acts are meant to make you feel that work of the intellect is meaningless." She was lecturing on the Crystal Palace as a monumental glass building, and began by alluding briefly to the anguish of speaking after the cataclysm. "We were shattered enough," she recalls. But in the midst of the talk, she realized how resonant were her quotations from the *Westminster Review*, about the way opaque walls were predicated on violence, but transparent walls were a symbol of the hope for peace.

At Kings College London, Ann Thompson was teaching *The Merchant of Venice* soon after September 11. In her course packet was an essay on the play by Avraham Oz, an Israeli leftwing scholar who discussed the stage history of various productions in Tel Aviv and Jerusalem, and related the staging to incidents of terrorism in the city. "Suddenly," Thompson says, "we found ourselves having the best seminar ever on the play."[19] At the University of Michigan, too, many faculty reported that "this has been the best semester of teaching that they have ever had." At UCLA, the provost of the College of Letters and Science suggested that "when you encounter a phenomenon as large as war, terror, or violence, you can connect to other parts of the human experience that yesterday or the day before you may not have thought of as relevant."[20]

At Mt. Holyoke, Sven Birkerts felt that "classes on poetry and creative writing are just as crucial" as classes on terrorism or Islam "for those trying to make sense of the unthinkable ... We have been given a context that makes the search for meaning obviously very important." He believes that his writing classes "have helped students grapple with the emotional turmoil that followed the attacks," but he also feels that he could have done something else, something more: "Maybe I didn't make it a specific teaching opportunity ... I wish I had been given a chance to rise to my role, to go beyond the subject."[21] But no one gives us these chances; we must make them, or seize them, for ourselves. In order to do so, we need to think and talk about our roles much more than we do.

When our lectures, seminars, and conferences are overtaken by public events as terrible and historic as those of September 11, our role is simple and almost inescapable. The event produces the desire to communicate, and insofar as we are able, we should go with that desire and facilitate it for a short while. Students themselves will begin to relate it to some part of the course, to try to understand it in terms we offer.

The more agonizing and ambiguous circumstances for the teacher of literature are those that fall between the public and the private, and yet are part of the community. What do you do if a student in your class or seminar is injured in an accident, or commits suicide, or dies of an overdose? What, if anything, should you say when a student's mother has been murdered? When his father is arrested for the crime and all the newspapers are head-lining the story? I have no answers for these questions, all of which have come up for my husband or myself, but I raise them to remind us that our role and our subject are not cleanly detached from the world, but messily entangled with it.

Conclusion: The Joy of Teaching Literature

Ending

As there are hospitality rituals for beginning a class and a course, there should also be some for saying farewell. The teacher needs to thank the students and the teaching assistants, and the slide projectionists and the video operators and the auditors; to wish everyone a pleasant holiday and safe journey. Often the final class is not the end of the term; there is a study break, or an exam, or a project due, and students need to know how to reach you. Your final text will shape the mood of your ending too; Michael Cadden believes that whatever text you end with is an invitation to some kind of closure – apocalyptic, nihilistic, or comic.

Moreover, the final class, writes Laura Nash, "should tally the score, review the semester's progress and the students' own development, perhaps return to the first class, and in short, hold the course up for examination and give it a finish. But the last class, like true scholarship, does not close the topic: the very final act is to break out of the frame, to direct attention to the next logical question, and most of all to leave the students not in panic but in perplexity."[1]

Of course, Nash is writing from a postmodern perspective that assumes that total closure and absolute clarity is not the goal of teaching. In a later essay, she returns to the question of "discovering the semester," and making full use of its chronology just as a writer or composer uses the culmination of the work of art. "This is the time," Nash suggests, "to focus on the open-ended philosophical question, the sticky textual problem that plagued later critics, the historical demise of the movement being studied, the observable or logical phenomenon that led to subsequent scientific or mathematic discoveries – whatever keeps the questioning alive and analytical skill relevant. In this way, the last class can attempt the rebirth of intellectual spirit that one hopes to encourage in students."[2]

In a real sense, teaching never ends, and the conclusion of the semester does not conclude the teacher–student relationship or the implicit contract. Many a time when I least expect it I have been startled to hear my name called in a ladies' loo in London, or a cafe in Montparnasse, and to see a familiar young face to which I can no longer put a name, and a happy student asking, "When are your office hours, Professor Showalter?" Sabbaticals too provide no immunity from requests for "small favors," like writing letters of recommendation to 15 law schools.

On the other hand, learning goes on after the end of a course, too, although final examinations may package it. "A teacher's real influence," writes Stuart Sherman, ". . . may run long past the last encounter, even into later generations. Much good comes from this not knowing, for a respect, even an affection for the work's uncertainties . . . For all the elaborate scheduling of causes – the syllabus, the class plan – there is no scheduling of effects. They happen when they happen. For all the teaching and the learning, there is, at the end of the hour and the year, no telling what will last."[3] One of the greatest joys of teaching is the letters from former students, years after the course, but never too late.

Teaching offers the illusion of a fountain of youth. It brings us into contact with young people and their enthusiasm and freshness, and allows us to have an impact on their lives. But the teaching persona we adopt when we are young fits less well as we age. Feminist professors, who have written most frankly about the personal elements of pedagogy, have discussed this aspect of the teaching self in detail. "Teaching is after all a 'work in progress,'" explain Phyllis Freeman and Jan Schmidt. "As we age and mature, so too must our teaching. Authentic teaching requires reflective practice. Teaching personalities that fit at twenty-five are not those that are authentic at fifty."[4]

One thing that happens to professors as they grow older is that they re-examine the compromises and accommodations they have made with their real beliefs for the sake of professional status and theoretical fashion. Lisa Ruddick has described a graduate seminar she taught at the University of Chicago during a period when she had just received tenure and was agonizing about breaking away from her own intellectual formation and indoctrination in certain "intellectual rules that were part of the dominant thinking," and that, in the name of "essentialism," forbade discussion of shared human concerns. Ironically, the seminar was called "Authenticity." "The readings I selected," Ruddick admits, "which contextualized the idea of authenticity historically, had a lot of truth to them, but they made no space for a state of mind that could be called, positively, authenticity . . . My goal in teaching such a course was to introduce students to the norms of the profession, as well as to show that I was myself up-to-date. But in subordinating everything to these goals, I was unwittingly teaching a kind of contempt for the search for an authentic life, a search that within the conceptual terms of the course could only look a little naïve."[5]

Diane Middlebrook thinks that her teaching has changed as she got older. "I used to think that I shared a world view with my students. That was sustained until my students were younger than my own daughter. Now I need to make links with what they know – and I wonder what it is that they know!" Developing a coherent teaching self is a life-long process. Lisa Jardine believes that "you cross a threshold when you feel entitled to tell it your way. The first ten years is about effacing yourself as a teacher. Then comes the time of feeling comfortable in your skin."

And what about the end of the teaching career itself? Some English professors regard it with deep gloom. Lionel Basney (Calvin College) meditated upon teaching as "an encounter with death," and wondered what he would do when he could no longer teach. "No one has told me this, but I suspect that the most frightening thing about retirement may be the sudden stillness of one's voice. A few of us, a very few, will be invited to schools and conferences to go on talking and put off the day of silence. Most of us will just have to go home and be silent. How will we get along with ourselves?"[6] Alvin Kernan, in his memoir *In Plato's Cave*, describes his first indirect lessons about teaching in the 1950s, when "a certain indifference to the students, mixed with a heavy manner of bored exasperation, was thought to set the right tone in the classroom." His account of the increasing bitterness of the generation that internalized those values makes enlightening, albeit sobering, reading.[7]

At Stanford, in 1910, English professor Melville Best Anderson composed and read a 54-page poem, "The Happy Teacher," for his retirement ceremony.[8] I hope no one reading this book will inflict such a revenge upon his or her department. But I hope too that for most, the joys of teaching literature, the joys of truly making a life in school, will predominate over the anxieties. May your dreams be sweet.

Notes

Preface

1 George Levine, "The Two Nations," *Pedagogy* 1 (Winter 2001): 10.
2 Ibid., 12.
3 Ibid., 17.
4 Kenneth E. Eble, *The Craft of Teaching*, 2nd edition (San Francisco: Jossey-Bass, 1988), 223.

Chapter 1 The Anxiety of Teaching

1 Isobel Armstrong, interview, February 5, 2002.
2 Wayne Booth, *The Vocation of a Teacher* (Chicago: University of Chicago Press, 1988), 253.
3 Jane Tompkins, *A Life in School: What the Teacher Learned* (Reading, Ma.; Addison-Wesley, 1996), 1.
4 Michael Berubé, "Dream a Little Dream," *The Chronicle Review* (September 21, 2001).
5 Tompkins, *A Life in School*, 1.
6 Ibid, 90.
7 Richard F. Elmore, "Foreword," *Education for Judgment: The Artistry of Discussion Leadership* (Boston: Harvard Business School Press, 1991), ix.
8 Norman Maclean, " 'This Quarter I am Taking McKeon': A Few Remarks on the Art of Teaching," *University of Chicago Magazine* 66 (January/February 1974): 8–12.
9 Jane Tompkins, "Pedagogy of the Distressed," *College English* 52 (October 1990): 655.
10 Tompkins, *A Life in School*, 86, 87, 88, 90.

11 Alvin Kernan, *In Plato's Cave* (New Haven: Yale University Press, 1999), 103.
12 Houston A. Baker, Jr., "1992: Local Pedagogy, or, How I Redeemed My Spring Semester," *PMLA* 115 (December 2000): 1939.
13 Michael Cadden, interview, October 30, 2001.
14 Alex Zwerdling, interview, August 2, 2001.
15 Lisa Jardine, interview, March 11, 2002.
16 Coppelia Kahn, "Mother," in *Changing Subjects*, ed. Gayle Greene and Coppelia Kahn (London and New York: Routledge, 1993), 164.
17 John Biggs, *Teaching for Quality Learning at University* (Buckingham and Philadelphia: Society for Research into Higher Education and Open University Press, 1999), 2.
18 Kenneth J. Eble, *The Craft of Teaching*, 2nd edition (San Francisco: Jossey-Bass, 1988), 3.
19 Parker J. Palmer, *The Courage to Teach: Exploring the Inner Landscape of a Teacher's Life* (San Francisco: Jossey-Bass, 1998), 142.
20 Ibid., 143.
21 "Frederick," in Jody D. Nyquist et al., "On the Road to Becoming a Professor," *Change* (May/June 1999): 24.
22 Marjorie Hope Nicolson, "A Generous Education" (1963), *PMLA* 115 (December 2000): 1867.
23 George Levine, "The Two Nations," *Pedagogy* 1 (Winter 2000): 7.
24 Gerald Graff, *Beyond the Culture Wars: How Teaching the Conflicts Can Revitalize American Education* (New York & London: W. W. Norton, 1992), 123.
25 Diana Laurillard, *Rethinking University Teaching*, 2nd edition (Milton Keynes: Open University Press), 4.
26 Booth, *The Vocation of a Teacher*, 242.
27 Stephen Greenblatt, "Letter in Response," *Pedagogy* 1 (Spring 2001): 436.
28 Kathy Overhulse Smith, "Teaching Our Mutual Friends," *Pedagogy* 1 (Spring 2001): 330.
29 Greenblatt, "Letter in Response," 436.
30 Paul Ramsden, *Learning to Teach in Higher Education* (London and New York: Routledge, 1992), 137.
31 Marlene A. Schiwy, "Saturating Language with Love," in *Wise Women: Reflections of Teachers at Midlife*, ed. Phyllis R. Freeman and Jan Zlotnik Schmidt (New York and London: Routledge, 2000), 28.
32 Richard Fraher, "Learning a New Art: Suggestions for Beginning Teachers," in *The Art and Craft of Teaching*, ed. Margaret Morganroth Gullette, (Cambridge: Harvard University Press, 1984), 117.
33 Booth, *The Vocation of a Teacher*, 219.
34 Palmer, *The Courage to Teach*, 49–50.
35 Frank Kermode, *Not Entitled*, (London: Flamingo, 1997), 175–7.
36 Tompkins, *A Life in School*, 119.
37 Patricia Hampl, "But Tell Me, Do You Like Teaching?" in Freeman and Zlotnik Schmidt, *Wise Women*, 63

38 Mark Edmundson, "On the Uses of Liberal Education as Lite Entertainment for Bored College Students," *Harper's* (September 1997): 39–40.

39 Eble, *The Craft of Teaching*, 13.

40 Larry Danson, interview, October 9, 2000.

41 Booth, *The Vocation of a Teacher*, 251.

42 Harvey C. Mansfield, "Grade Inflation: It's Time to Face the Facts," *The Chronicle Review* (April 6, 2001).

43 Wilbert J. McKeachie, *Teaching Tips: Strategies, Research, and Theory for College and University Teachers*, 10th edition (Boston: Houghton Mifflin, 1999), 85. This edition has chapters by teachers from the Open University as well as American universities.

44 Joseph Lowman, *Mastering the Techniques of Teaching* (San Francisco: Jossey-Bass, 1995), 185.

45 Ibid., 194.

46 Booth, *The Vocation of a Teacher*, 211.

47 Ibid., 219.

48 Frederick Morgan Padelford, "Retrospect and Prospect," *PMLA* 115 (December 2000): 1834.

Chapter 2 Theories of Teaching Literature

1 George Levine, "The Two Nations," *Pedagogy* 1 (2001):14.

2 Terry Eagleton, *Literary Theory: An Introduction*, 2nd edition (Oxford: Blackwell, 1996), 9.

3 Peter Widdowson, *Literature* (London and New York: Routledge, 1999), 45.

4 W. B. Carnochan, "The English Curriculum: Past and Present," *PMLA* 115 (December 2000): 1960.

5 Eagleton, *Literary Theory*, 27.

6 Ibid., 27.

7 Ibid., 43.

8 Frances Smith Foster, "African-American Study, Now and Then," *PMLA* 115 (December 2000): 1967.

9 James Engell and David Perkins, eds., *Teaching Literature: What is Needed Now* (Cambridge: Harvard University Press, 1988).

10 Leslie A. Fiedler, "Teaching English: The Two Traditions," *ADE Bulletin* 65 (1980): 6–10.

11 John Schilb, "Preparing Graduate Students to Teach Literature," *Pedagogy* 1 (Fall 2001): 512.

12 Wilbert J. McKeachie, *Teaching Tips: Strategies, Research, and Theory for College and University Teachers*, 10th edition (Boston: Houghton Mifflin, 1999), 10.

13 Linda B. Nilsen, *Teaching at Its Best* (Bolton, Ma.: Anker, 1998), 13.

14 B. S. Bloom, ed., *Taxonomy of Educational Objectives. Handbook I: Cognitive Domain* (London: Longman, 1956).

15 Nilsen, *Teaching at Its Best*, 13.

16 Paul Ramsden, *Learning to Teach in Higher Education* (London and New York: Routledge, 1992), 134.

17 Roger Kuin, "Poststructuralism: Teaching the Amoretti," in *Approaches to Teaching Shorter Elizabethan Poetry*, ed. Patrick Cheney and Anne Lake Prescott (New York: Modern Language Association, 2000), 171–2.

18 Patrick Brantlinger, *Who Killed Shakespeare?* (New York and London: Routledge, 2001), 40.

19 Robert Scholes, *Textual Power: Literary Theory and the Teaching of English* (New Haven: Yale University Press, 1985), 39.

20 Robert Scholes, *The Crafty Reader* (New Haven and London: Yale University Press, 2001), 215.

21 Geoffrey Petty, *Teaching Today*, 2nd edition (Cheltenham: Stanley Thornes Ltd., 1998), 346.

22 These learning objectives are inspired in part by those in *The Practice of University History Teaching*, ed. Alan Booth and Paul Hyland (Manchester and New York: Manchester University Press, 2000), 6–7. Thanks to my husband, English Showalter, for brainstorming with me on this topic.

23 Paulo Freire, *Pedagogy of the Oppressed*, trans. Myra Bergman Ramos (London: Penguin, 1996), 53.

24 Barbara Riebling, "Contextualizing Contexts," in *Day Late, Dollar Short: The Next Generation and the New Academy*, ed. Peter C. Herman (Albany: State University of New York Press, 2000), 182.

25 Sharon Cowley, quoted in Riebling, *Day Late*, 180.

26 Cary Nelson, "A Theorized Poetry Course," in *Teaching Contemporary Theory to Undergraduates*, ed. Dianne F. Sadoff and William E. Cain (New York: Modern Language Association, 1994), 179–94.

27 Alvin Kernan, *In Plato's Cave* (New Haven: Yale University Press, 1999), 104.

28 David Denby, *Great Books* (New York: Simon and Schuster, 1996), 41–2.

29 Ibid., 123.

30 Oliver Arnold, interview, November 15, 2000.

31 Jeff Nunokawa, interview, November 13, 2000.

32 Martin Bickman, *Approaches to Teaching Melville's "Moby-Dick"* (New York: Modern Language Association, 1985), ix.

33 Gerald Graff, *Professing Literature: An Institutional History* (Chicago and London: University of Chicago Press, 1987), 258, 262.

34 David H. Richter, ed., *Falling into Theory: Conflicting Views on Reading Literature* (Boston: Bedford, 1994), vii.

35 Louis Menand, in Richter, *Falling into Theory*, 109.

36 Levine, "The Two Nations," 11.

37 William Pritchard, *English Papers* (St. Paul: Graywolf Press, 1985), 184.

38 Frederick Crews, *Postmodern Pooh* (New York: North Point Press, 2001), iii.
39 Edward L. Rocklin, " 'An Incarnated Act': Teaching Shakespeare," *Shakespeare Quarterly* 41 (Summer 1990): 153.
40 Camille Paglia, *Sex, Art, and American Culture* (London: Penguin, 1992), 237, 120, 279, 127.
41 Lionel Basney, "Teacher: Eleven Notes," *The American Scholar* 71 (Winter 2002): 80.
42 Jyl Lynn Felman, *Never a Dull Moment: Teaching and the Art of Performance* (London and New York: Routledge, 2001), xviii, 15.
43 Kenneth E. Eble, *The Craft of Teaching*, 2nd edition (San Francisco: Jossey-Bass, 1988), 18.
44 Nilsen, *Teaching at Its Best*, 76.
45 Parker J. Palmer, *The Courage to Teach: Exploring the Inner Landscape of a Teacher's Life* (San Francisco: Jossey-Bass, 1998), 10.
46 Parker J. Palmer, *To Know as We Are Known* (San Francisco: Harper, 1993), x, xi, xvi, 71, 74.
47 Ibid., 85, 86, 115.
48 Stephen D. Brookfield, *Becoming a Critically-Reflective Teacher* (San Francisco: Jossey-Bass, 1995), 72–3.
49 David Perkins, "Taking Stock After Thirty Years," in Engell and Perkins, *Teaching Literature*, 112.
50 Victoria Thorpe Miller, "*Personal Recollections of Joan of Arc* in Today's Classroom," in *Making Mark Twain Work in the Classroom*, ed. James S. Leonard (Durham, N.C. and London: Duke University Press, 1999), 57.
51 John Dewey, *How We Think* (Lexington, Mass., D. C. Heath, 1933), 35.
52 Freire, *Pedagogy of the Oppressed*, 61.
53 McKeachie, *Teaching Tips*, 6.
54 Anne L. Bower, "Sharing Responsibility for American Lit," in *The Canon in the Classroom*, ed. John Alberti (New York: Garland, 1995), 221–40.
55 Palmer, *The Courage to Teach*, 121–3.
56 Rachel C. Livsey, in collaboration with Parker J. Palmer, *The Courage to Teach: A Guide for Reflection and Renewal* (San Francisco: Jossey-Bass Publishers, 1998), 32–3.
57 Steven Gould Axelrod, "Teaching *Moby-Dick* to Non-English Majors," in Bickman, *Approaches to Teaching Melville's "Moby-Dick"*, 74.
58 Carl Woodring, *Literature: An Embattled Profession* (New York: Columbia University Press, 1990), 182.
59 Rollo Walter Brown, *Harvard Yard in the Golden Age* (New York: Current Books, 1948), 72.
60 Michael White, "The First Hobbit," *The Sunday Times* (December 9, 2001): *News Review*, 1.
61 Carolyn Heilbrun, *When Men Were the Only Models We Had* (Philadelphia: University of Pennsylvania Press, 2001), 11, 7.
62 Frank Kermode, *Not Entitled* (London: Flamingo, 1997), 242.

63 Gayle Pemberton, in *Wise Women: Reflections of Teachers at Midlife*, ed. Phyllis R. Freeman and Jan Zlotnik Schmidt (New York & London: Routledge, 2000), 170.
64 Barbara Johnson, "Deconstruction, Feminism, and Pedagogy," in Engell and Perkins, *Teaching Literature*, 70.
65 William H. Pritchard, *English Papers: A Teaching Life* (Saint Paul: Graywolf Press, 1995), 89–95.
66 Richard E. Miller, *As If Learning Mattered: Reforming Higher Education* (Ithaca and London: Cornell University Press, 1998), 95.
67 David Garvin, "Barriers and Gateways to Learning," in *Education for Judgment*, ed. C. Roland Christensen et al., (Boston: Harvard Business School Press, 1991), 12.

Chapter 3   Methods of Teaching Literature

1   Marshall Gregory, "Curriculum, Pedagogy, and Teacherly Ethos," *Pedagogy* 1 (Winter 2001): 75.
2   Walter J. Ong, "The Human Nature of Professionalism," *PMLA* 115 (December 2000): 1913.
3   Douglas L. Howard, "American Psychos: Insanity, Academe, and Other Special Topics," *Chronicle Career Network*, January 25, 2002, http://chronicle.com/cgi2-bin/printable.cgi.
4   David Damrosch, "The Mirror and the Window: Reflections on Anthology Construction," *Pedagogy* 1 (Winter 2001): 207.
5   Kenneth E. Eble, *The Craft of Teaching*, 2nd edition (San Francisco: Jossey-Bass, 1988), 72.
6   Jyl Lynn Felman, *Never a Dull Moment: Teaching and the Art of Performance* (London and New York: Routledge, 2001), 158.
7   Stuart Sherman, "Teaching in Time," *Academe* (September/October 1996): 37.
8   Ann Thompson, "Research-Led Teaching? Or Teaching-Led Research?" *English Subject Newsletter* (February 2001): 7.
9   Wayne Booth, *The Vocation of a Teacher* (Chicago: University of Chicago Press, 1988), 211.
10 Laura L. Nash, "The Rhythms of the Semester," in *The Art and Craft of Teaching*, ed. Margaret Morganroth Gullette (Cambridge: Harvard University Press, 1984), 70–87.
11 Steven Gould Axelrod, "Teaching *Moby-Dick* to Non-English Majors," in *Approaches to Teaching Melville's "Moby-Dick,"* ed. Martin Bickman (New York: Modern Language Association, 1985), 74.
12 See Jeffrey Wolcowitz, "The First Day of Class," in Gullette, *Art and Craft of Teaching*, 10–24.
13 Felman, *Never a Dull Moment*, 4, 123.

149

14   Jeff Nunokawa, interview.

15   David Denby, *Great Books* (New York: Simon and Schuster, 1996), 39.

16   Abby J. Hansen, "Establishing a Teaching-Learning Contract," *Education for Judgment*, 127.

17   Michael Berubé, "Dream a Little Dream," *The Chronicle Review* (September 21, 2001).

18   See, for example, Heather Fry, Steve Ketteridge, and Stephanie Marshall, *A Handbook for Teaching and Learning in Higher Education* (London: Kogan Page, 1999), 86.

19   Donald A. Bligh, *What's the Use of Lectures?* (Exeter: Intellect, 1998), 14, 10.

20   Martin Bickman, "Teaching Teaching: Construction and Reflection in the Classroom," *Reader: Essays in Reader-Oriented Theory, Criticism, and Pedagogy* 33/34 (Spring/Fall, 1995): 90.

21   Parker J. Palmer, *To Know as We Are Known* (San Francisco: Harper, 1993), 33.

22   Michael Berubé, "Teaching to the Six," *Pedagogy* 2 (Winter 2002).

23   Interview with Donald Hall, *Professions*, 262.

24   Emily Toth, *Ms. Mentor's Impeccable Advice for Women in Academia* (Philadelphia: University of Pennsylvania Press, 1997), 90.

25   Phil Baty, "Star Turn: Rob Pope," *THES* (June 25, 1999): 30–1.

26   Wilbert J. McKeachie, *Teaching Tips: Strategies, Research, and Theory for College and University Teachers*, 10th edition (Boston: Houghton Mifflin, 1999), 214.

27   Richard M. Felder, "How About a Quick One?" *Chemical Engineering Education* 26 (Winter 1992): 18.

28   Eble, *The Craft of Teaching*, 16.

29   Quoted in Alan Booth and Paul Hyland, *The Practice of University History Teaching* (Manchester: Manchester University Press, 2000), 112.

30   David Garvin, "Barriers and Gateways to Learning," in *Education for Judgment*, ed. C. Roland Christensen, Daniel A. Garvin, and Ann Sweet (Boston: Harvard Business School Press, 1991), 11.

31   Quoted in Bickman, *Approaches to Teaching Melville's "Moby-Dick,"* 3.

32   C. Roland Christensen, "The Discussion Teacher in Action: Questioning, Listening, and Response," in Christensen, *Education for Judgment*, 153–72.

33   "Christensen, University Professor, Dies at 80," *Harvard University Gazette* (September 16, 1999).

34   William Gleason, interview November 9, 2000.

35   Donald A. Bligh, *What's the Use of Lectures?* (Exeter: Intellect, 1998), 19.

36   Andrew Bennett and Nicholas Royle, *Introduction to Literature, Criticism and Theory*, 2nd edition (Harlow: Prentice Hall Europe, 1999), 261.

37   Terry Eagleton, *Literary Theory: An Introduction*, 2nd edition (Oxford: Blackwell, 1996), 38.

38 John Schild, "Preparing Graduate Students to Teach Literature," *Pedagogy* 1 (Fall 2001): 513.

39 Clark Hulse, "Elizabethan Poetry in the Postmodern Classroom," in *Approaches to Teaching Shorter Elizabethan Poetry*, ed. Patrick Cheney and Anne Lake Prescott (New York: Modern Language Association, 2000), 67.

40 I recommend Phil Race and Steve McDowell, *500 Computing Tips for Teachers and Lecturers*, 2nd edition (London: Kogan Paul, 1999).

41 Paul Ramsden, *Learning to Teach in Higher Education* (London and New York: Routledge, 1992), 181.

42 Ibid., 98.

43 Richard E. Miller, *As If Learning Mattered* (Ithaca & London: Cornell University Press, 1998), 209.

44 Eble, *The Craft of Teaching*, 163.

Chapter 4   Teaching Poetry

1 Frank H. Ellis, *PMLA* 115 (December 2000): 2045.

2 Anne Lake Prescott, in *Approaches to Teaching Shorter Elizabethan Poetry*, ed. Patrick Cheney and Anne Lake Prescott (New York: Modern Language Association, 2000), 61.

3 Stephen Regan, "Poetry, Please," http://www.rhul.ac.uk/ltsn/english/Newsletter/archive/Vol_1_2/regan.htm.

4 Dinitia Smith, "The Eerily Intimate Power of Poetry to Console," *New York Times*, October 1, 2001; Andrew Motion, "Voices from Adversity," *The Guardian*, October 20, 2001.

5 Billy Collins, "The Companionship of a Poem," *The Chronicle Review* (November 23, 2001).

6 Robert Scholes, "Reading Poetry: A Lost Craft," in *The Crafty Reader* (New Haven and London: Yale University Press, 2001), 1–75.

7 Patrick Cheney, in Cheney and Prescott, *Approaches to Teaching Shorter Elizabethan Poetry*, 54.

8 Marjorie Perloff and Robert van Hallberg, "A Dialogue on Evaluation in Poetry," in *Professions*, ed. Donald E. Hall (Urbana and Chicago: University of Illinois Press, 2001), 87.

9 Jonathan Arac, "An Introductory Texts and Theory Course," in *Teaching Contemporary Theory to Undergraduates*, ed. Dianne Sadoff and William E. Cain (New York: Modern Language Association, 1994), 174.

10 Diane Middlebrook, interview, October 4, 2001.

11 Julia Reinhard Lupton, "Sex and the Shorter Poem" in Cheney and Prescott, *Approaches to Teaching Shorter Elizabethan Poetry*, 105, 103.

12 Heather Dubrow, "Teaching Genre," in Cheney and Prescott, 153–4.

13 Regan, "Poetry, Please."

14 Roland Greene, "The Experimental and the Local," in Cheney and Prescott, 258.

15 George Klawitter, "A Guide to *Paradise Lost*, Book 9," in *Approaches to Teaching Milton's Paradise Lost*, ed. Galbraith M. Crump (New York: Modern Language Association, 1986), 107–11.

16 Michael M. Levy, "Paradise Lost in Northern Wisconsin," in Crump, *Approaches to Teaching Milton's Paradise Lost*, 56, 57.

17 Hugh Kenner, "Reading Poetry," in *Teaching Literature: What is Needed Now*, ed. James Engell and David Perkins (Cambridge: Harvard University Press, 1988), 3, 6–7.

18 Camille Paglia, *Sex, Art, and American Culture* (London: Penguin, 1992), 127.

19 Donald R. Howard, "The Idea of a Chaucer Course," in *Approaches to Teaching Chaucer's "Canterbury Tales,"* ed. Joseph Gibaldi (New York: Modern Language Association, 1980), 57–62.

20 Harold Bloom, *How to Read and Why* (London: Fourth Estate, 2001), 73.

21 Ibid., 74, 142.

22 Chris Hedges, "Poetry as Armor Against Highs and Lows of Life," *New York Times* (May 18, 2001): C2.

23 Collins, "The Companionship of a Poem."

24 Diane Middlebrook, interview, October 4, 2001.

25 Cary Nelson, "A Theorized Poetry Course," in Sadoff and Cain, *Teaching Contemporary Theory*, 180, 188.

26 Diana E. Henderson, "Learning to Love the Star Lover: Teaching 'Astrophel and Stella,'" in Cheney and Prescott, *Approaches to Teaching Shorter Elizabethan Poetry*, 200.

27 Caroline McManus, "The Multiple Readerships of Elizabethan Poetry," in Cheney and Prescott, 121.

28 Clark Hulse, "Elizabethan Poetry in the Postmodern Classroom," in Cheney and Prescott, 69–70.

29 Frank Kermode, *Not Entitled* (London: Flamingo, 1997), 197.

30 McManus, "The Multiple Readerships," 200.

31 Dubrow, "Teaching Genre," 153–4.

32 John Webster, in Cheney and Prescott, *Approaches to Teaching Shorter Elizabethan Poetry*.

33 Roland Greene, in Cheney and Prescott, 261.

34 Arac, in Sadoff and Cain, *Teaching Contemporary Theory*, 173.

35 Irene Tayler, "Blake at MIT," in *Approaches to Teaching Blake's "Songs of Innocence and Experience,"* ed. Robert F. Gleckner and Mark L. Greenberg (New York: Modern Language Association, 1989), 81–3.

36 Sandra M. Gilbert, "Teaching Plath's 'Daddy' to Speak to Undergraduates," *ADE Bulletin* 76 (Winter 1983): 38–42.

37 Jewell Speares Brooker, "When Love Fails: Reading *The Waste Land* with Undergraduates," in *Approaches to Teaching Eliot's Poetry and Plays*, ed. Brooker (New York: Modern Language Association, 1988), 103–8.

38 Donald R. Howard, "The Idea of a Chaucer Course," in *Approaches to Teaching Chaucer's "Canterbury Tales,"* ed. Joseph Gibaldi (New York: Modern Language Association, 1980), 57–62.
39 John Fleming, interview, November 28, 2001.

Chapter 5   Teaching Drama

1 Kenneth E. Eble, *The Craft of Teaching*, 2nd edition (San Francisco: Jossey-Bass, 1988), 51.
2 R.V. Cassill and Richard Bausch, *The Norton Anthology of Short Fiction*, 6th edition (New York: Norton, 2000), 1640.
3 J. L. Styan, *PMLA* 115 (December 2000): 2020; *The Dramatic Experience* is published by Cambridge University Press.
4 James N. Loehlin, "On Your Imaginary Forces Work: Shakespeare in Practice," in *Teaching Shakespeare through Performance*, ed. Milla Cozart Riggio (New York: Modern Language Association, 1999), 286.
5 Milla Cozart Riggio, "Introduction," *Teaching Shakespeare through Performance*, 1.
6 David Bevington and Gavin Witt, "Working in Workshops," in Riggio, *Teaching Shakespeare*, 169, 170, 175, 180.
7 Michael Shapiro, "Improvisational Techniques for the Literature Teacher," in Riggio, *Teaching Shakespeare*, 186.
8 Quoted in Riggio, "Introduction," 12.
9 Lois Potter, "Teaching Shakespeare: The Participatory Approach," in Riggio, *Teaching Shakespeare*, 235, 243.
10 Ibid., 236, 238.
11 Ralph Alan Cohen, "Original Staging and the Shakespeare Classroom," in Riggio, *Teaching Shakespeare*, 99.
12 Stephen Orgel, "Why Did the English Stage Take Boys for Women?" in Riggio, *Teaching Shakespeare*, 101, 111, 103.
13 Edward L. Rocklin, "'An Incarnated Act': Teaching Shakespeare," *Shakespeare Quarterly* 41 (Summer 1990): 61–2.
14 Oliver Arnold, interview, November 15, 2000.
15 Larry Danson, interview, October 9, 2000.
16 Michael Cadden, interview, October 30, 2001.
17 Ann Thompson, "*King Lear* and the Politics of Teaching Shakespeare," *Shakespeare Quarterly* 41 (1990): 539.
18 Graham Aitken, "Reading Plays," in *Studying Literature: A Practical Introduction*, ed. Aitken et al. (London: Harvester/Wheatsheaf), 176.
19 Robert N. Watson, "Teaching Shakespeare: Theory vs. Practice," in *Teaching Literature: What is Needed Now*, ed. James Engell and David Perkins (Cambridge: Harvard University Press, 1988) 125.

20 Jyl Lynn Felman, *Never a Dull Moment: Teaching and the Art of Performance* (London and New York: Routledge, 2000).

21 Michael J. Conlon, "Literature and Performance in Eighteenth-Century England," *Teaching the Eighteenth Century* (1995): 18–19.

Chapter 6   Teaching Fiction

1 W. B. Carnochan, "The English Curriculum Past and Present," *PMLA* 115 (December 2000): 1960.

2 Quoted by J. J. Wilson, *PMLA* 115 (December 2000): 1990.

3 Carolyn Heilbrun, *Writing a Woman's Life* (New York, 1988), 114.

4 Jerome McGann, "Reading Fiction/Teaching Fiction: A Pedagogical Experiment," *Pedagogy* 1(Winter 2001):144.

5 James S. Leonard, ed., *Making Mark Twain Work In the Classroom* (Durham, N.C. and London: Duke University Press, 1999), 1, 7–8.

6 McGann's syllabi and comments are included in "Reading Fiction", 143–65.

7 Peter V. Conroy, Jr., "The Enlightenment Novel," *Teaching the Eighteenth Century* (1991): 3.

8 Steven Gould Axelrod, "Teaching *Moby-Dick* to Non-English Majors," in *Approaches to Teaching Melville's "Moby-Dick,"* ed. Martin Bickman (New York: Modern Language Association, 1985) 67–74.

9 Interview with Jeff Nunokawa, November 13, 2000.

10 Conroy, "The Enlightenment Novel," 43.

11 Sanford E. Marovitz, "Teaching *Moby-Dick*: A Freshman Honors Course," in Bickman, *Teaching Melville's "Moby-Dick,"* 56–65.

12 William Shurr, "*Moby-Dick* as Tragedy and Comedy," in Bickman, 32, 34.

13 Lisa Berglund, "Samuel Johnson and the Eighteenth Century," *Teaching the Eighteenth Century* (1999): 57. Berglund credits the idea to Terry Belanger of the University of Virginia.

14 Crystal Downing, *PMLA* 115 (December 2000): 2045.

15 Robert Alter, *The Pleasures of Reading in an Ideological Age* (New York and London: Norton, 1996), 176.

16 Brad Haseman, "Playing the Crowded House," in *Lecturing: Case Studies, Experience and Practice*, ed. Helen Edwards(London: Kogan Page, 2001), 68.

17 Ben Knights, *From Reder to Reader* (New York and London: Harvester, 1992), 36–7.

18 Daniel Menaker, interview, July 26, 1994, distributed by the *New Yorker* to teachers of literature.

Chapter 7   Teaching Theory

1 Sandra Gilbert, interview, in *Professions*, ed. Donald E. Hall (Urbana and Chicago: University of Illinois Press, 2002), 252.

2 Terry Eagleton, *Literary Theory*, 2nd edition (London: Blackwell, 1996), 190.

3 Robert Alter, *The Pleasures of Reading* (New York: Norton, 1996), 3.

4 Jeffrey Williams, "The Posttheory Generation," in *Day Late, Dollar Short: The Next Generation and the New Academy*, ed. Peter C. Herman (Albany: State University of New York Press, 2000), 25–43.

5 Martin Bickman, "Teaching Teaching," *Reader: Essays on Reader-Oriented Theory, Criticism and Pedagogy* 33/34 (Spring/Fall 1995): 86.

6 D. G. Myers, "On the Teaching of Literary Theory," *Philosophy and Literature* 18 (October 1994): 326–36.

7 Donald G. Marshall, "Doxography versus Inquiry: Two Ways of Teaching Theory," in *Teaching Contemporary Theory*, ed. Dianne F. Sadoff and William E. Cain (New York: Modern Language Association, 1994), 81.

8 D. N. Rodowick, "Gray is Theory (Except in Black or White or Color); or, the Paradoxes and Pleasures of Film Theory," in Sadoff and Cain, *Teaching Contemporary Theory*, 253–4.

9 Beverly Lyon Clark, et al., "Giving Voice to Feminist Criticism," in Sadoff and Cain, 127.

10 Dianne F. Sadoff, "Frameworks, Materials, and the Teaching of Theory" in Sadoff and Cain, 16.

11 Susan B. Lanser, "The T-Word: Theory as Trial and Transformation of the Undergraduate Classroom," in Sadoff and Cain, 63.

12 Diana Fuss, "Accounting for Theory in the Undergraduate Classroom," in Sadoff and Cain, 104.

13 John Kucich, "Confessions of a Convert: Strategies for Teaching Theory," in Sadoff and Cain, 44.

14 Lanser, "The T-Word," 57.

15 Fuss, "Accounting for Theory," 105.

16 Dianne Sadoff, "Frameworks, Materials, and the Teaching of Theory," in Sadoff and Cain, 15.

17 Andrew Bennett and Nicholas Royle, "Preface to the first edition," *Introduction to Literature, Criticism, and Theory*, 2nd edition (Harlow: Pearson, 1999), vii.

18 Interview with Mark Hanson, November 8, 2000.

19 Fuss, "Accounting for Theory," 109.

20 Kucich, "Confessions," 46.

21 Downing, "Ancients and Moderns," in Sadoff and Cain, 32.

22 Lanser, "The T-Word," 57–68.

23 Gary Waller, "Polylogue," in Sadoff and Cain, 97.

24 Lynette Felber, "Everything You Always Wanted to Know," in Sadoff and Cain, 72. The essay is "Recipes for Reading: Summer Pasta, Lobster à la Riseholme, and Key Lime Pie," *PMLA* 104 (1989): 340–7.

25 Sandra Grayson, "Teaching Realism as Theory," in Sadoff and Cain, 115.

26 Laurie A. Finke, "The Pedagogy of the Depressed," in Sadoff and Cain, 159.

27 See http://lcdweb.cc.purdue.edu/~felluga/syn22Ag00.html

Chapter 8   Teaching Teachers

1   Sue Lonoff, "Using Videotape to Talk about Teaching," *ADE Bulletin*, 118 (Winter 1997): 13.
2   Richard M. Felder, "Teaching Teachers to Teach: The Case for Mentoring," *Chemical Engineering Education* 27 (1993): 176.
3   Martin Bickman, "Teaching Teaching: Construction and Reflection in the Classroom," *Reader: Essays in Reader-Oriented Theory, Criticism, and Pedagogy* 33/34 (Spring/Fall 1995): 85.
4   Kenneth E. Eble, *The Craft of Teaching*, 2nd edition (San Francisco: Jossey-Bass, 1988), 201–2, 204.
5   Jody D. Nyquist and Jo Sprague, "Thinking Developmentally about TAs," in *The Professional Development of Graduate Teaching Assistants*, ed. M. Marincovitch, J. Prostiko and F. Stout (Bolton, Ma.: Anker), 63–6.
6   Diana Laurillard, *Rethinking University Teaching*, 2nd edition (London: Open University Press, 2001), 3.
7   Louis B. Barnes, C. Roland Christensen, and Abby J. Hansen, eds, *Teaching and the Case Method* (Boston: Harvard Business School Press, 1994).
8   Bickman, "Teaching Teaching." 95.
9   Ibid., 93.
10 Jerome McGann, "Reading Fiction/Teaching Fiction: A Pedagogical Experiment," *Pedagogy* 1 (Winter 2001): 158.
11 Eble, *The Craft of Teaching*, 213.

Chapter 9   Teaching Dangerous Subjects

1   James S. Leonard, *Making Mark Twain Work in the Classroom* (Durham, N.C. and London: Duke University Press, 1999), 1.
2   See Robert Felger, "*Native Son* and Its Readers," and Farah Jasmine Griffin, "On Women, Teaching, and *Native Son*," both in *Approaches to Teaching Wright's "Native Son*," ed. James A. Miller (New York: Modern Language Association, 1997).
3   Jeffrey Berman, "Syllabuses of Risk," *The Chronicle Review* (February 15, 2002), B7.
4   Jeffrey Berman, *Surviving Literary Suicide* (Amherst: University of Massachusetts Press), 1.
5   Ibid., 25.
6   Ibid., 1.
7   If your university does not provide such material, it is easily obtained on the internet. The National Mental Health Organization (http://www.nmha.org/inforctr/factsheets/81.cfm) has a list of warning signs, advice to friends, and telephone hotlines and information numbers in the US.

8 Elizabeth Benedict, "Introduction to the second edition," *The Joy of Writing Sex* (New York: Owl, 2002). Thanks to Liz Benedict for an advance copy.
9 Martha C. Nussbaum, *Cultivating Humanity* (Cambridge: Harvard University Press, 1997), 204.

Chapter 10   Teaching Literature in Dark Times

1 Louise Rosenblatt, *Literature as Exploration* (New York: Modern Language Association, 1995), 16, 124.
2 James M. Banner and Harold C. Cannon, *The Elements of Teaching* (New Haven: Yale University Press, 1997), 35.
3 Wilbert J. McKeachie, *Teaching Tips: Strategies, Research, and Theory for College and University Teachers*, 10th edition (Boston: Houghton Mifflin, 1999), 333.
4 James Hilton, *Goodbye, Mr. Chips* (London: Hodder and Stoughton, 2001), 95, 96, 97.
5 Jefferson B. Fletcher, "Our Opportunity" (1915), *PMLA* 115 (December 2000): 1781.
6 Jyl Lynn Felman, *Never a Dull Moment: Teaching and the Art of Performance* (London and New York: Routledge, 2001), 20.
7 Carolyn Shrodes, "The Scholars and the Anti-Self," *ADE Bulletin* 26 (1970): 4–11.
8 Hyungji Park, *PMLA* 115 (December 2000): 2039.
9 Jerry Aline Flieger, "Growing up Theoretical," in *Changing Subjects*, ed. Gayle Greene and Coppelia Kahn (London and New York: Routledge, 1993), 255.
10 Stuart Sherman, "Teaching in Time," *Academe* (September/October 1996): 37.
11 Lisa Ruddick, "The Near Enemy of the Humanities is Professionalization," *The Chronicle Review* (November 23, 2001).
12 Vijay Seshadri, "Whitman's Triumph," *The American Scholar* 71 (Winter 2002): 136, 140.
13 Douglas L. Howard, "Teaching Through Tragedy," *The Chronicle Career Network* (September 20, 2001). (www.Chronicle.com/jobs/2001/09/2001092001c.htm)
14 Ibid.
15 Karla Jay, "Teaching as Healing at Ground Zero," *The Chronicle Review* (October 12, 2001).
16 Carolyn Foster Segal, "The Solace of Literature," *The Chronicle Review* (October 5, 2001).
17 William Germano, "The Way We Read Now," *The Chronicle Review* (October 5, 2001).
18 Julie Crosby, "Theatre of the Absurd," http://www.chronicle.com/jobs/2001/11/2001110502c.htm.

19 Ann Thompson, interview, February 20, 2002.
20 Ana Marie Cox, "The Changed Classroom, Post-September 11," *Chronicle of Higher Education* (October 26, 2001).
21 Sven Birkerts, "The Changed Classroom, Post September 11," *Chronicle of Higher Education* (October 26, 2001).

Conclusion: The Joy of Teaching Literature

1 Laura N. Nash, "The Rhythms of the Semester," in *The Art and Craft of Teaching*, ed. Margaret Morganroth Gullette (Cambridge: Harvard University Press, 1984), 87.
2 Laura N. Nash, "Discovering the Semester," in *Education for Judgment*, ed. C. Roland Christensen, David A. Garvin, and Ann Sweet (Boston: Harvard Business School Press, 1991), 247–8.
3 Stuart Sherman, "Teaching in Time," *Academe* (September/October 1996): 39.
4 Phyllis R. Freeman and Jan Zlotnick Schmidt, "Introduction," *Wise Women: Reflections of Teachers at Midlife* (New York and London: Routledge, 2000), 3.
5 Lisa Ruddick, "The Near Enemy of the Humanities is Professionalization," *The Chronicle Review* (November 23, 2001).
6 Lionel Basney, "Teacher: Eleven Notes," *The American Scholar* 71 (Winter 2002): 81.
7 Alvin Kernan, *In Plato's Cave* (New Haven: Yale University Press, 1999).
8 W. B. Carnochan, "The English Curriculum: Past and Present," *PMLA* (December 2000): 1959.

Index

abortion 129
Abrams, M. H. 65
active learning *see* student-centered teaching
ADE Bulletin 9
Adler, Mortimer 40–1
administration 59–60
Adventures of Huckleberry Finn (Twain) 89, 125
African-American studies 17–18, 23
Aitken, Graham 86–7
Alter, Robert 94, 104
Anderson, Melville Best 143
Angels in America (Kushner) 129
anxiety 3–4, 20
  coverage 12–13
  dreams 1–3
  evaluation 19–20
  grading 17–19
  isolation 9–11
  lack of training 4–9
  performance 13–17
  teaching versus research 11–12
Arac, Jonathan 65, 73–4
Armstrong, Isobel 2, 7, 20, 39, 52, 87, 92, 125–6, 139
Arnold, Oliver 30, 48, 84, 85

Assessing Student Learning in Higher Education (Brown) 58
assessment 17–19, 57–9, 123–4
assignments 98–101, 109
Association of American Colleges (AAC) 8
Association of American University Professors (AAUP) 8
Atkinson, Ti-Grace 30
Atwood, Margaret 94, 115
Axelrod, Steven 37, 47, 91

Bachner, Sally 114
Bad Sex Prize 128
Baker, Houston 6
banking model *see* subject-centered teaching
Banner, James M. 132
Barnes, Louis B. 113–14
Barthes, Roland 22
Barton, John 80
Basney, Lionel 33, 143
Bausch, Richard 79–80
Bayley, John 33–4
Beckermann, Bernard 80, 82
Beckman, Karen 114
Beer, Gillian 10
beginnings 97–8, 117–18

Benedict, Elizabeth 128
Benjamin, Walter 115
Bennett, Andrew 56, 107
Berglund, Lisa 93
Berman, Jeffrey 126–7
Berubé, Michael 2–3, 48, 50
Bevington, David 81
Beyond the Culture Wars (Graff) 31
Bickman, Martin 30–1, 49–50, 104,
    106–7, 112, 116, 123
Biggs, John 8
Birkerts, Sven 139
Blackboard software 57
Blake, William 74–5
Bligh, Donald A. 49, 55
Bloom, B. S. 25
Bloom, Harold 69
Booth, Wayne 2, 12, 14, 17, 19, 20,
    46
Bower, Anne L. 36
Bradbury, Malcolm 48–9
Brantlinger, Patrick 25–6
Bride of Lammermoor, The (Scott) 90
Brooker, Jewel Spears 76–7
Brookfield, Stephen 35
Brooks, Cleanth 62
Brower, Reuben 39–40
Brown, George 58
Bryn Mawr 53
Bull, Joanna 58
Burgess, Anthony 99–100
Butler, Judith 104
buzz groups 52

Cadden, Michael 6–7, 84–6, 129, 141
Cain, William E. 106
Cambodian invasion 133–4
Cannon, Harold 132
Canterbury Tales, The (Chaucer) 72–3,
    74, 77
Carby, Hazel 10
Carnegie Corporation 8
Carnochan, W. B. 88
Chaucer, Geoffrey 72–3, 74, 77–8

Cheney, Patrick 64–5
Christensen, C. Roland 53–4, 113–14
Chronicle of Higher Education 8, 9,
    51
Citizen Kane 110
Clockwork Orange, A (Burgess)
    99–100
close reading 55–6, 98–9
Cohen, Ralph Alan 83
College English 5, 8, 9
Collins, Billy 63, 64, 70
color 39, 47
commonplace books 71
comparison, poetry 73–4
conflicts 31–2
Conlon, Michael 87
Conroy, Peter V. 90–1, 92
content 12–13, 27, 28
conversion experience 99–100
course coverage 12–13
Craft of Teaching, The (Eble) 8
creative writing, poetry 71–3
Crews, Frederick 31–2
crises 131–40
critical pedagogy 28–9
Crosby, Julie 138
Cross, Amanda 89

"Daddy" (Plath) 75–6
Damrosch, David 43
dangerous subjects 113–14, 120–1,
    125–30
Danson, Larry 17, 43, 44, 45–6, 56–7,
    84, 85
Danto, Arthur 138
de Man, Paul 39
Dearing Report 9–10
Denby, David 29–30, 47
Dessen, Alan 80
Dessen, Cynthia 80
Developing University English
    Teaching (DUET) 111
Dewey, John 36
Dickinson, Emily 74

discussion 53–5
  controlling 119–21
  opening questions 118–19
Douglass College 10
Downing, Crystal 93–4
Downing, David 108
drama 79–87
dreams 1–3
Dubrow, Heather 66, 72
Dylan, Bob 74

Eagleton, Terry 21–3, 56, 103
Eble, Kenneth ix, 8, 16–17, 33, 44,
  52, 59, 79, 112–13, 124
eclectic teaching theories 37–8
Edmundson, Mark 16
Edson, Margaret 50, 135
Eighteenth-Century Studies 9
electronic classroom 56–7
elegies 66
Eliot, George 93–4
Eliot, T. S. 42, 68, 76–7
Ellis, Frank 62
Elmore, Richard 4
endings 101–2, 141–3
English Subject Centre 9, 111
Eugenides, Jeffrey 127–8
evaluations 19–20, 124
explication de texte 55–6, 98–9
explicit sexual language 128–30

Faludi, Susan 115
Felber, Lynette 109
Felder, Richard 52
Felluga, Dino Franco 109–10
Felman, Jyl Lynn 33, 44, 47, 87, 133
fiction 88–90
  active learning 93–4
  beginnings 97–8
  course structure 92–3
  endings 101–2
  length 90–2
  middles 98–101
  narrator and teacher 94–6

themes and learning objectives
  96–7
Fiedler, Leslie 24
Finke, Laurie 109
first class 46–8
Fish, Stanley 11, 31–2, 104
Fitzgerald, Scott 100–1
Fleming, John 77–8
Fletcher, Jefferson 133
Flieger, Jerry Aline 134
Ford, Ford Madox 33
Fraher, Richard 13–14
Franzen, Jonathan 128
Freeman, Phyllis 142
Freire, Paulo 5, 27–8, 36
Freud, Sigmund 14
Funaroff, Sol 70–1
Fuss, Diana 106, 107, 108

Gardner, Howard 87
Garvin, David 41, 53
genres, poetry 66–7
Germano, William 138
Gilbert, Miriam 80
Gilbert, Sandra 75–6, 103
Gilman, Sander 10
Gleason, William 36, 55, 94
Glossary of Literary Terms (Abrams) 65
Goodbye, Mr. Chips (Hilton) 132
Gordimer, Nadine 94
Gordon, D. J. 15
grade inflation 17–18, 57
grading 17–19, 57–9, 124
Graff, Gerald 11, 31
Grayson, Sandra 109
Greenberg, William 46
Greenblatt, Stephen 12, 13, 84, 104
Greene, Gayle 79
Greene, Roland 66–7, 73
Gregory, Marshall 42

Hampl, Patricia 16
Handmaid's Tale, The (Atwood) 94,
  115

Hansen, Abby 48, 113–14
Hanson, Mark 55, 108
Harry Potter and the Sorceror's Stone (Rowling) 123
Harvard 17–18, 40, 53, 111–12
Haseman, Brad 94–5
Haugen, Kristine 72–3, 74
Heilbrun, Carolyn 39, 89
Henderson, Diana E. 71
Herrick, Robert 72
High Fidelity (Hornby) 115
Hilton, James 132
Homer 138
Hornby, Nick 115
housekeeping 59–60
Howard, Donald 68, 77, 78
Howard, Douglas 42–3, 136
Howard, Ron 48
Huckleberry Finn 89, 125
Hulse, Clark 71

Iliad 138
implicit contract 47–8
Institute for Learning and Teaching (ILT) 10, 111
intellectual conviction 29–31
internet
    and breakdown of isolation 9
    commonplace books 71
    and course coverage 12–13
    literary theory 109–10
    new technology 56–7
isolation 9–11, 20

Jameson, Frederick 104
Jamison, Kaye Redfield 126, 127
Jardine, Lisa 7, 39, 55, 129, 143
Jay, Karla 136–8
Johnson, Barbara 39
Joy of Writing Sex, The (Benedict) 128
July's People (Gordimer) 94

Kahn, Coppelia 7
Kalstone, David 39–40

Keeley, Howard 101
Kennedy assassination 133
Kenner, Hugh 67
Kermode, Frank 15, 39, 71–2
Kernan, Alvin 6, 29, 143
Kessler, Milton 32–3, 68
Key Words (Williams) 109
Kittredge, George Lyman 38
Klawitter, George 67
Knights, Ben 95
Kucich, John 107, 108
Kuin, Roger 25
Kushner, Tony 129

Lanser, Susan 106, 107, 108–9
Laurillard, Diana 11, 113
learning objectives 24–7
Leavis, F. R. 22–3
lecturing 48–52, 68, 77
Leonardi, Susan 109
Levenson, Jill L. 83
Levertov, Denise 70
Levin, Harry 93
Levine, George vii, viii, 11, 21, 31
Levy, Michael M. 67
Literary Review 128
literary theory 103–7
    fear of 107
    in practice 107–9
    teaching 109–10
literature
    definitions 21–2
    eclectic teaching theories 37–8
    goals of teaching 22–4
    learning objectives 24–7
    student-centered teaching 27, 35–7
    subject-centered teaching 27–32
    teacher-centered teaching 27, 32–5
    teaching personae 38–41
    see also drama; fiction; poetry
Liu, Alan 109
Loehlin, James N. 80–1

Lonoff, Sue 111–12
"Love Song of J. Alfred Prufrock, The"
(Eliot) 68
Lowman, Joseph 18–19
Lupton, Julia Reinhard 66

McGann, Jerome 89–90, 124
Mack, Maynard 6
McKeachie, Wilbert 8, 18, 24, 36, 52,
132
Maclean, Norman 4–5, 89
McManus, Caroline 71, 72
Mandel, Barrett 10
Mansfield, Harvey 18
marking 17–19, 57–9, 124
Marovitz, Sanford 93
Marshall, Donald G. 105
Mastering the Techniques of Teaching
(Lowman) 18–19
"Medusa's Head" (Freud) 14
Melville, Herman 91, 93
memorization 69–70
men
poetry 62
teaching personae 38–9
Menaker, Daniel 98
Menand, Louis 31
Mentor, Ms. 51
metaphors 66
methods *see* teaching methods
microcosm 36–7, 91
Middlebrook, Diane 65–6, 68, 69, 70,
72, 127, 143
Middlemarch (Eliot) 93–4
Miller, J. Hillis 24
Miller, Richard 58
Miller, Victoria Thorpe 35
Milton, John 67, 74, 87, 110
Moby-Dick (Melville) 91, 93
modeling 55–6, 85
Modern Language Association (MLA)
8–9, 11
Moore, Lorrie 129
Motion, Andrew 63

Mousley, Andy 107
Myers, D. G. 104–5

narrative 94–6, 110
Nash, Laura 46, 141–2
Native Son (Wright) 125
Nelson, Cary 28–9, 70–1
New Criticism 23, 55–6, 62, 64, 106
new technology 56–7
Nicolson, Marjorie Hope 11
Nilsen, Linda 25, 34
*Norton Anthology of English Literature,
The* 13, 43
novels *see* fiction
Nunokawa, Jeff 30, 47, 89, 91, 92
Nussbaum, Martha 130
Nyquist, Jody 113

O'Neill, Michael 82
Ong, Walter 42
Open University 111
Oresteia, The 29
Orgel, Stephen 83
Oz, Avraham 139

Paglia, Camille 32–3, 68
Palmer, Parker J. 9, 10, 15, 34–5,
36–7, 50
Pamela (Richardson) 90–1
Paradise Lost (Milton) 67, 74, 87, 110
Park, Hyungji 134
parody 72–3
Pechter, Edward 79
Pedagogy 9
Pemberton, Gayle 39
Pendlebury, Malcolm 58
performance anxiety 13–17
performance teaching 32–4
drama 80–7
Perkins, David 35
Perloff, Marjorie 65
personae 38–41, 47–8, 117–18, 142
Phelps, William Lyon 22
Plath, Sylvia 75–6, 127

Playing Shakespeare (Barton) 80
plays 79–87
poetics 65–6
poetry 62–5, 75–8
  student-centered methods 68–75
  subject-centered methods 65–7
  teacher-centered methods 67–8
Poirier, Richard 39–40
political conviction 28–9
Pope, Rob 52
portfolios 73
possession-by-memory 69
Postmodern Pooh (Crews) 31–2
posttheory generation 103–7
Potter, Lois 80, 82–3
precepts 113–17
  beginning 117–18
  classroom management 122–3
  controlling discussion 119–21
  course planning, pacing and
    continuity 121–2
  ending 123–4
  grading 124
  opening questions 118–19
  student course evaluations 124
preparation 42–6
Prescott, Anne Lake 62
Princeton 29, 57, 84–6, 101, 113–15
Pritchard, William 31, 39–40
Project to Improve College Teaching
  8

Quality Assurance Agency (QAA) 111
questioning 53–5
Quinn, Alice 69–70

race 120–1, 125–6
Ramsden, Paul 13, 25, 58
reading 26, 55–6, 86
reading aloud 67–8
recitation 70–1, 78
reflection 8, 35, 79
Regan, Stephen 62–3, 66
religion 129

research 11–12, 44–5
Richard, I. A. 23
Richard, Jessica 54, 56
Richardson, Samuel 90–1
Richter, David 31
Riggio, Milla Cozart 81
Rocklin, Edward L. 32, 83–4
Rodowick, D. N. 105–6
Rosenblatt, Louise 132
Rowling, J. K. 123
Royal Holloway College 9, 111
Royle, Nicholas 56, 107
Ruddick, Lisa 135, 142–3

Sadoff, Dianne F. 106, 107
Schild, John 56
Schmidt, Jan 142
Scholes, Robert 26, 63–4, 72
Scott, Sir Walter 90
Sedgwick, Eva Kosofsky 104
Segal, Carolyn Foster 138
September 11, 63, 135–9
Seshadri, Vijay 135–6
Sexton, Anne 127
sexual language 128–30
Shakespeare, William 80–1, 82, 83–5
Shakespeare Quarterly 9, 80
Shapiro, Michael 82
Sherman, Stuart 45, 134, 142
short stories 88, 92
Showalter, English 43–4
Shrodes, Carolyn 133–4
Shurr, William H. 93
SMART 26
Smith, Dinitia 63
Smith, Kathy Overhulse 12
Smith, Stephanie 58
sonnets 66, 72
spiritual theory of teaching 34–5, 50
Sprague, Jo 113
stage fright 13–17
stand-up comedy 32–3
Stephanson, Anders 47
Stiffed (Faludi) 115

student-centered teaching 8, 27, 35–6, 38
  discussion 54
  drama 79
  fiction 93–4
  lectures 52
  poetry 68–75
  teaching from the microcosm 36–7
student evaluations 19–20, 124
Students from Hell 14–15
Styan, J. L. 80
subject-centered teaching 27–8
  conflicts 31–2
  critical pedagogy 28–9
  intellectual conviction 29–31
  poetry 65–7
suicide 126–8
Summers, Lawrence 17–18
Swander, Homer (Murph) 80

Tayler, Edward 30
Tayler, Irene 74–5
teacher-centered teaching 27
  performance 32–4
  poetry 67–8
  spiritual journey 34–5
teachers, training 4–9
teaching assistants 111–24
Teaching and the Case Method (Barnes, Christensen and Hansen 113–14
Teaching Contemporary Theory to Undergraduates (Sadoff and Cain) 106
Teaching Literature 24
teaching methods 42, 61
  first class 46–8
  grading 57–9
  housekeeping 59–60
  leading discussions 53–5
  lecturing 48–52
  modeling 55–6
  new technology 56–7
  poetry 64–78
  preparation 42–6

teaching personae 38–41, 47–8, 117–18, 142
Teaching for Quality Learning at University (Biggs) 8
Teaching Shakespeare through Performance 80–1
Teaching-the-Conflicts 31–2
teaching theories 27
  definitions 21–2
  goals 22–4
  objectives 24–7
  see also eclectic teaching theories; student-centered teaching; subject-centered teaching; teacher-centered teaching
Teaching Tips (McKeachie) 8
textual triage 12–13
theory *see* literary theory
Thompson, Ann 45, 63, 86, 129, 139
Times Higher Education Supplement 8, 9
To Know as We Are Known (Palmer) 34–5
Tolkien, J. R. R. 38–9
Tompkins, Jane 2, 3, 5–6, 15–16, 131
Toth, Emily 51
training 4–9, 111–24
Trilling, Lionel 39
"Troilus and Criseyde" (Chaucer) 77–8
Twain, Mark 89, 125

Understanding Poetry (Brooks and Warren) 62, 63–4
University College London 22
"Unpacking My Library" (Benjamin) 115

Vendler, Helen 24
video clips 60, 82, 83, 96
Vietnam War 134
Virgin Suicides (Eugenides) 127–8

Waller, Gary 109
Waste Land, The (Eliot) 76–7

Watson, Robert 87
Web *see* internet
Webster, John 73
Welles, Orson 110
West, Cornel 17–18
"What the Thunder Said" (Funaroff)
    70–1
Whitehead, Alfred North 35–6
Whitman, Walt 135–6
Who Will Run the Frog Hospital
    (Moore) 129
Williams, Jeffrey 104
Williams, Raymond 109
Williamson, George 19
Witt, Gavin 81

Wofford, Suzanne 6
women, teaching personae 39, 50
women's studies 23
Woodring, Carl 37–8
Wright, Richard 125
writing, on poems 73
writing poetry 71–3
W;t (Edson) 50, 135

Yale 5–7, 62, 64

Zimmerman, Bonnie 51
Zwerdling, Alex 7, 46, 89, 91, 92–3,
    94